BELL'S BOOK OF TRICKS

BELL'S BOOK OF TRICKS

cards, coins, handkerchiefs and paper

by Patrick Page

Bell Publishing Company
New York

CONTENTS

Tricks with Cards

In many card tricks you will require a spectator to 'cut the cards'. This means that you want him to remove approximately half the pack of cards from the top and place them to one side. When you 'complete the cut' this means that you pick up the remaining cards and place them on top of the packet of cards which the spectator has placed aside. This 'cutting the cards' and 'completing the cut' is very important in the presentation of card tricks, because there are many card tricks which depend entirely on the fact that the cards have been 'cut' properly.

Arrange Cards in Suits

It is not generally known that a pack of cards can be cut as often as you like and the original order of the cards will remain unaltered. Perhaps a practical demonstration will explain this more fully. Take a pack of cards and arrange the whole fifty two cards in order from the top down. Start with the Ace of Clubs and place it face up on the table. Now place the Two of Clubs face up on top of the Ace. Now place the Three of Clubs face up on top of the Two. Now carry on like this until you have the whole thirteen cards of the Club suit one on top of the other, the last card being, of course, the King of Clubs. Now start on the Spades suit. Place the Ace of Spades on top of the King of Clubs, face up. On top of the Ace place the Two of Spades then the Three and so on until you have the thirteen Spade cards on top of the Clubs. Repeat this with the Heart suit and then the Diamond suit so that eventually you have all fifty two cards face up in one packet, and all in perfect rotation.

Cut and Cut Again

Turn this pack of cards face down on the table. Remember, they are all in order. Now cut the cards and complete the cut.

Have you done that?

Yes?

All right. do it again. Yes! Cut the cards and complete the cut. Now do it again another six times if you like. At this stage, most people would imagine that the cards will by now be well and truly mixed up, but in fact they will not be mixed at all. Turn the pack face up and spread the cards face up along the table and you will see that they are still in perfect order, Ace to King etc. It may be – in fact it probably will be – that the first card, that is to say, the top card of the pack will no longer be the Ace of Clubs, but whatever card is now the first card, *all the cards which follow it will be in perfect rotation.*

This is an important principle to remember because many good card tricks are based on this principle alone, and the first card trick in this book actually utilises this principle.

THE RED AND BLACK
CARD MYSTERY—PART ONE
To prepare

For this effect you will require to separate the red cards from the black cards. All the red cards should be in the bottom half of the deck and all the black cards in the top half. They need not be in rotation or in any particular order, just make sure that all the red cards are in the bottom half and all the black are in the top half. Needless to say, the spectators should not be aware of this fact.

To present

Hold the cards in both hands and spread them out in a sort of fan fashion and ask someone to select a card. When this person has taken one of the cards, make a mental note of which half of the pack the card was selected from. Ask the spectator to look at the card and remember it.

Now instruct the spectator to replace the card in the pack and, as you say this, separate

2

the pack into two packets but make sure that you separate the pack somewhere in the half from which the card *was not selected.* In short, if the spectator removes a card from the red half of the deck, then you must make certain that the card is returned to the black half of the pack.

Square the cards up into a neat packet and place them face down on the table, and ask someone to cut the cards, and complete the cut. Once this has been done, you can if you wish point out that a card has been selected, returned to the pack and the cards have been cut and that it should be impossible for anyone to know the exact whereabouts of the Selected Card. If you now pick up the cards and spread them faces towards you, you will find that there is one red card sitting right in the middle of a bunch of black cards. *This red card is the Selected Card.*

Remove this red card and place it face down on the table in front of you. Ask the spectator who selected the card to name the card he selected. When he does so, turn the card face up with a flourish.

We have used the principle to hide the fact that the cards were pre-arranged. If a spectator ever suspects that a pack of cards has been arranged in some sort of order, the fact that you allow him to cut the cards as often as he likes will allay those suspicions.

In the foregoing card trick, the fact that the cards have been cut makes no difference to the order of the cards. The Selected Card, which in this instance was a red card, was simply transferred from the red half of the pack to the black half of the pack, and no amount of cutting will alter the fact that one red card is in the middle of a bunch of black cards. Now let us take the same card trick a step further.

THE RED AND BLACK
CARD TRICK—PART TWO

Let us assume that you are performing the Red and Black Card Mystery and you have reached the stage where you spread the cards with their faces towards you and are looking for the Selected Card.

At this point, instead of looking for the Selected Card, separate the cards where the red cards meet the black cards and return them to their original position so that all the red cards are in one half of the deck and all the black cards are in the other. There will be one odd card in the wrong half as before and this card, will, of course be the Selected Card.

After you have replaced the cards in their original order, remove this Selected Card and place it face down on the table as before. If you stop to think at this moment you will realise that what you have done is rearrange the cards in their original order *before you have actually finished the trick you are performing.*

This means that you are all set to repeat the effect if you wish. Now there is a very old saying among magicians: "Never repeat the same trick before the same audience". The reason for this is simply that if a spectator knows exactly what you are going to do, then he is more attentive and more likely to spot something he shouldn't. If you have already shown him the trick once, he will be in a position to study much more carefully your actions during the repetition of the effect. In the present instance, although you are in a position to repeat the effect, we are going to vary it enough to throw anyone off the scent.

At the conclusion of the previous effect, pick up the card from the table and replace it in the pack, making sure that it is returned to the right half. Now hold the cards faces towards you and spread them out in a fan fashion. Separate the pack into two so that you are holding all the black cards in the right hand and all the red cards in the left hand. Place the black cards face down on the table to your right. Spread the red cards out fan fashion face down and ask a spectator to take one from the pack.

When the spectator has selected a card, place all the red cards face down on the table to your left and pick up the black cards and have a spectator select a card from the black half. Again, when the spectator has selected a card place the black half on the table to your right.

The position now is that all the black cards are in one packet on the right side of the table and all the red cards are in one packet on the left side of the table. Both packets are face down. Two spectators are holding cards.

Ask the first spectator to replace his card in the centre of the other half of the pack. This means that although he is holding a red card you ask him to replace it in the black half of the pack. Now ask the spectator who is holding the black card to replace his card in the red half of the pack. Once this has been done place one half of the pack on top of the other half, and ask someone to cut the cards and complete the cut.

Once this has been done, you explain what has happened. Two spectators have Selected Cards and replaced them into a different part of the pack, and the cards after being reassembled have been cut. At this stage, once again, no one can possibly know where the two Selected Cards are actually situated in the pack. Pick up the pack and spread them faces towards you, and when you do so you will once again see a single red card in the middle of a bunch of black cards, but you will also see one black card in the middle of a bunch of red cards. *These two cards are the cards which were selected by the two spectators.*

Remove these two cards from the pack and place them face down on the table. Ask both spectators to name their cards and when they do so turn both cards over simultaneously, one in each hand.

5

SLEIGHT OF HAND WITH CARDS

If you ever aspire to being a good card magician you are going to have to learn sleight of hand. Millions and millions of words have been written on the subject of sleight of hand with cards, but one of the most important items discussed in all these millions of words is the problem of having a card selected, returned to the centre of the pack, and somehow controlled by the card magician so that it is brought to the top of the pack. One of the most popular methods of controlling a card to the top of the pack is by means of a peculiar piece of sleight of hand called —

THE HINDU SHUFFLE
To Present

We will assume that you have already had a card selected. The spectator is holding the card. You have the pack in your left hand. With the right fingers and thumb, draw out the bottom half of the pack. This is known as undercutting the pack. Offer to the spectator the cards that remain in the left hand and ask him to replace his card on top of those you are holding in the left hand.

When he has done so, bring the right hand over the left hand and, as you place the cards in the right hand on top of those in the left hand, the right fingers and thumb take hold of the selected card. The left fingers and thumb take a grip of some of the cards on top of the

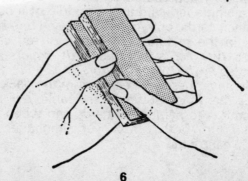

packet in the right hand and pull them off. The right hand at the same time, pulls backwards, taking the Selected Card with it, under the packet it is holding. The cards that were drawn off by the left fingers are allowed to drop on to the packet of cards held in the left hand.

If the whole procedure is performed smoothly it will look as if you have simply deposited some cards from the top of the right hand packet on top of the Selected Card. In fact you have stolen the Selected Card from the top of the left hand packet under cover of depositing those cards.

The position now is that the Selected Card is on the bottom of the right hand packet. Bring the right hand packet over the left hand as before and with the left fingers and thumb draw off some more cards from the top of the right hand packet on to the top of the left hand packet.

This is repeated again and again, the left fingers always drawing off a few cards from the top of the right hand packet and depositing them on top of the left hand packet. You are, in reality, continually under cutting the pack.

Continue to do this until you have only one card left in the right hand. This card will be the bottom card of the right hand packet which is the Selected Card and it is placed on top of the pack.

You will have to study the description of the Hindu Shuffle slowly to enable you to understand it clearly, but if you really want to learn sleight of hand with cards, I am quite sure that you have already studied it several times.

THE GLIDE

This is another sleight which can be used for many different effects. The object of the Glide is to place a card on the table face down, say, the Two of Clubs, and when the card is turned face up it will be seen to have changed to another card.

To Present

Hold the pack of cards in the left hand as in the illustration. The left thumb on one side of the pack and the four fingers on the other side. Notice that the fingers are projecting quite a way beyond the edge of the pack. Show the face card, the Two of Clubs to the spectators then turn the left hand over so that the face of the card is facing the table top. As you do so, the second third and fourth fingers of the left hand curl inwards on to the face of the

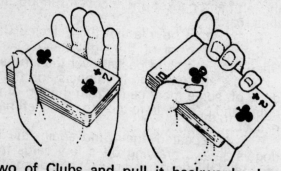

Two of Clubs and pull it backwards about half an inch.

The right hand approaches and apparently pulls the Two of Clubs from the face of the pack. In fact, it is pulling the second card from the pack. The Two of Clubs has been drawn back a little to allow the right fingers to make contact with the second card. This second card is placed face down on the table. When it is turned face up, it is another card. The Two of Clubs is still on the bottom of the pack.

Again, as in the Hindu Shuffle, this sleight should be practised until you can do it smoothly and with natural actions.

Before we describe the Top Stock Shuffle we had better make sure that you can give a pack of cards an ordinary shuffle. Hold the cards with the thumb at one end and the four fingers at the other, in the right hand. The left hand reaches up and the left thumb draws off a card on to the left fingers. Now repeat this, continually drawing cards off into the left hand until there are no more cards in the right hand. That's it! You can shuffle a pack of cards.

THE MAGNETISED CARDS
To Prepare

This is a spectacular effect with a pack of cards and employs a special card. The picture will explain what this special card looks like. It is made by cutting three sides of a square in the centre of a card and folding the centre piece up at right angles to the rest of the card. This card is then pasted on to the back of another card. If you do not wish to spoil a new pack of cards use the two Jokers which are usually supplied with most packs today.

The projecting piece of card can now be folded flat to its original position. When required, just bend the card slightly by applying pressure to the face of the card with the finger-tips and the little flap will pop up out of its resting place.

To perform the Magnetised Cards at the

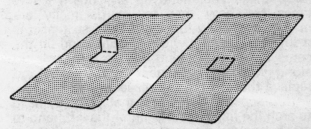

conclusion of some other card effects it is necessary to have the flap card inside the card case. This is a simple matter, if, when you commence performing, you remove the packet from the card case and leave the flap card behind in the card case. When you have finished performing, place the cards back into the case, and as you place the pack back into your pocket, pause, and say: "Wait a minute, there was one other thing I wanted to show you." As you say this, tip the cards out of the case again making sure that you add the flap card to them.

To Present

Pick up the flap card and, holding it with its face to the spectators with both hands, bend it back and forth slightly so that the flap pops out on the back of the card. Explain that the idea is to place one of the cards face up on the palm of your hand. You demonstrate by placing the flap card face up on the palm of your left hand and as you do so, grip the flap tightly between the first and second fingers. The problem now, you explain, is to try and tuck as many cards as possible under the edge of this card between the card and your palm.

You now proceed to place as many cards as you can all around and under the edges of the flap card. About fifteen will be enough. Once you have the cards in position, tell the spectators that you are going to magnetise the cards.

Having said this you proceed to turn your hand over slowly and as this is done the cards cling to your palm. When the palm is facing the floor, shake your hand up and down a few times to show that the cards really are magnetised. Now turn your hand so that it is palm up again and with the right hand lift the cards off the left palm. Square the cards up along with the remainder of the pack and replace them in the card case.

In practice you will find that you may have to arch the fingers and palm of the left hand to create enough pressure to make sure that the cards will be held in position. If you decide you wish to perform this effect before a larger audience on a small platform for instance, there is no need to resort to having the flap card in the card case. Simply have it lying on your table and at one point place the pack on the table on top of the flap card, and when you pick up the pack again the flap card will be added to it.

A more spectacular finale can be added to the Magnetised Cards if you are performing on a platform. Instead of removing the cards from the left palm with the aid of the right hand, simply explain that you will demagnetise the cards and as you say this, toss the cards up into the air, releasing your grip on the flap card of course. The cards will fly upwards and flutter down to the floor. This finale is only suitable where no one is likely to start picking up the cards before you do.

THE NEXT CARD WILL BE YOURS

The method used to achieve this effect is very old and very simple indeed. In fact, it would be safe to assume that most of you who are interested in card tricks already know the principle involved, so you will appreciate the little subtlety we have included to throw the knowing ones off the scent.

To Present

To start with you must secretly make a note of the card on the bottom of the pack. Let's say it is the Ace of Diamonds. Make a mental note of it and remember that the Ace of Diamonds is on the bottom of the pack. Have someone select a card and after he has done so, square up the pack and place it on the table. Ask the person who has selected the card to look at it and remember it and place it on top of the pack which is sitting on the table.

Once the spectator has placed the card on top of the pack, ask him to cut approximately half of the pack from the top and place it to one side. Once he has done this, ask him to place what was originally the bottom half of the pack and place it on top of the packet he has placed aside.

What he has done in effect is to bury his card somewhere in the centre of the pack. You should now point out that it should be impossible to find his card because no one knows exactly at which point in the pack he has placed his card.

No doubt you have realised by now that the Ace of Diamonds, which was originally on the bottom of the pack, is now sitting on top of the Selected Card. If you now start picking cards from the top of the pack one at a time and place them aside FACE UP you will eventually come to the Ace of Diamonds. When this happens, the very next card will be the Selected Card, but don't stop. Carry on turning the cards face up and placing them aside until you have gone five or six cards past the Selected Card, then stop.

The cards you have been placing aside should not be in a neat pile, just place them on the table haphazardly so that you can still see the Selected Card face up in the pile.

At this point you should stop dealing cards, and say: "The next card I turn over will be the Selected Card".

Now the person who has selected the card will know that you have already gone past his card, and he will probably think that the trick has gone wrong. Hold your hand above the table with the forefinger outstretched as if you are about to drop it on to the top of the pack then suddenly drop your hand on the the Selected Card and turn it over so that it is now face down.

The fact that you have been turning cards over all the time will lead the spectator to think that the card you are about to turn over is the one on the top of the pack, but you turn the tables on him by actually turning over the selected card, which is lying face up on the table.

THE THREE CARD TRICK
The Effect
The Three Card Trick is probably the most famous card trick of all time. People who have never seen it, discuss it as if they had. The plot is one of the simplest. Three cards are shown to a spectator. The centre card of the three cards

is a picture card, usually a Queen, which accounts for the trick sometimes being called Find the Lady. The three cards are placed on the table and the spectator is invited to point to the one which he thinks is the Queen. No matter which card he points to, he is always wrong. This is repeated several times, and the spectator can never win.

To Prepare

For this effect you will require three cards alike. You will probably find it easier to secure three Jokers, as any other three cards all alike will perhaps ruin three packs of cards. You also need one other card – a Queen. Take the Queen and with a sharp pair of scissors, cut a piece

 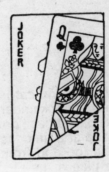

from the Queen as shown in the illustration and paste it on to the face of one of the other cards in the position shown. Your preparations are now complete. Place the card with the Queen on it, face up, on the table and place the other two Jokers face up on top of it.

To Present

Pick up the three cards and hold them in the right hand as in the picture. The left hand fingers reach under the three cards held in the right hand and slide out the bottom card a little more than half way until the Queen shows a little. Point out that you have three cards and

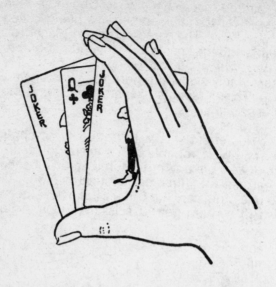

that the centre card is a Queen. Push the Queen card back under the other two cards and turn the packet face down. Now deal the three cards one at a time face down on to the table from the top and from right to left. This procedure places the Queen card on your right. The other two cards are, of course, Jokers.

Ask the spectator to POINT to the card which he thinks is the Queen. The reason the spectator is instructed to POINT is that you must not at any time give him the opportunity to pick up the cards. Always say POINT to the card. Usually the spectator will point to the centre card. If he does so, turn this card face up and show that it is a Joker. Place this card back on to the table face down and place the other Joker on top of it also face down and on top of these two cards place the Queen card also face down. Do not at any time show the faces of these two cards. You are now ready to repeat the effect.

Pick up the three cards and holding them as before, spread the bottom card out to the left showing part of the Queen again. Square the cards up, turn them face down and deal them out face down on the table as before. Once again you ask the spectator to point to the card he thinks is the Queen. If he points to the centre card again, you simply show it to him and proceed as before. If he points to the card on your left which is the Joker turn it over to show it is a Joker and replace it on the table face down. Drop the other Joker face down on top of it and then the Queen card also face down on top of it and start again.

Should he point to the actual Queen card, don't pick it up immediately. Look at the spectator in surprise and say: "I thought you would have picked this one". As you say this, pick up the centre card and turn it over to show it is a Joker. Hold this card in your left hand face down and slide it under the left side of the Queen card and pick up both cards and show the faces of both cards to the spectator.

Due to the way you are holding the cards, the first Joker will be covering the Queen but exposing the side of the Joker. It will look as if you are holding two Jokers. Lower your hand so that you are holding the cards face down. Pick up the other Joker with the right hand and insert it between the other two cards in the left hand, saying: "You should have picked this one". Notice that you do not show that this third card is a Joker. The reason for this is that you are now ready to repeat the effect again if you wish.

An alternative presentation, which gives the effect a climax, is to show the third Joker and when someone says, as they will: "Where's the Queen?" you reach into your jacket pocket and produce the Queen. This is a duplicate Queen which you had placed in your pocket before performing the effect.

THE VANISHING CARDS
The Effect
The Vanishing Cards is similar in principle to the Three Card Trick in that it uses a similar type trick card. A glance at the illustrations will reveal this to you. The effect, briefly, is as follows. Five playing cards are shown and dropped into a hat or a box on the table. Two cards are removed from the box. The spectators are invited to name the three cards which are left in the box. After the spectators have named the three cards which they think have been left in the box, the performer picks up the box and turns it over to show that it is empty. The three cards have vanished from the box. Reaching into his inside jacket pocket the performer produces the three missing cards.

To Prepare
We suggest that you use cards which are completely different in colours, suits and values, but for illustration purposes we intend to use five cards of the same suit, namely, the Ace, Two, Three, Four and Five of Spades. Place the Ace of Spades face up on the table and glue to this Ace a piece of the Two of Spades, then a piece of the Three of Spades and finally a piece of the Four of Spades. The finished article will look like the picture.

Now turn this Prepared Card over and place it on the table face down and on to the back of this card glue a duplicate Ace of Spades. Once this card has dried out, turn it over and hold it face up in the left hand and place the Five of Spades on top of it also face up.

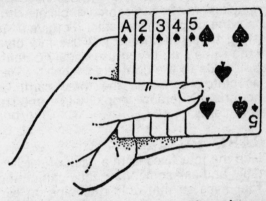

Hold the cards in the left hand as shown on page 33 and with the left thumb push the Five of Spades over to your right. This will expose the indices of the Ace, Two, Three and Four underneath.

To Present

Hold the cards in this position for a few moments while you draw attention to the fact that you are holding five cards. Now drop the cards into a box which is sitting on the table. Ask the spectators if they can remember all five cards. Reach into the box and remove the Prepared Card, but as you do so turn it over so that the Ace side is showing. Draw attention to the fact that it is indeed the Ace that you are removing from the box. Place this card aside.

The spectators will assume that there are still four cards in the box. In fact by removing the Ace you have also removed the Two, Three and Four.

Now reach into the box and remove the Five which is the only card left in the box. Once again draw attention to which card you are in fact removing from the box, and that there are still three cards left in the box. Now ask the spectators if they can remember the three cards which are left in the box. After they have tried to name them, lift up the box and show that it is empty.

The three cards which you remove from your pocket are of course three duplicate cards which were placed there earlier. Forgive us for repeating that you should not use five cards from the same suit. If you use widely differing cards, it adds to the confusion when you ask the spectators to name the three cards left in the box. Different people will remember different cards.

A CARD PUZZLE

Place the four fives from a pack of cards on the table and ask someone if they can arrange the four fives so that only four pips on each card show. When they have tried and failed, take the four fives and arrange them as shown in the illustration showing that four fives can be made into four fours in just a matter of seconds.

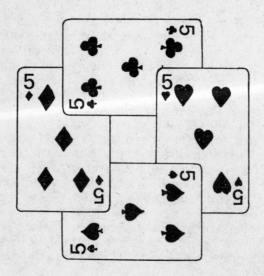

AN OPTICAL ILLUSION

The title of this effect describes how you explain the effect after you have performed it and not how the effect is actually achieved. This is an effect which should be a little more interesting than most in that it uses two sleights already described in this book, namely The Hindu Shuffle and The Glide.

To Present

To begin with a spectator selects a card from the pack and returns it to the centre. By means of The Hindu Shuffle the Selected Card is controlled by you to the top of the pack. Now that the Selected Card is on top of the pack, spread the top few cards to the right until three cards can be separated from the others. Take these three cards and transfer them, one at a time, from the top of the pack to the bottom and as you do so point out that any card could in fact be the Selected Card. Once the three cards have been transferred from the top to the bottom of the pack the Selected Card will be the *third card from the bottom of the pack*.

Hold the pack with the thumb on one side and the four fingers on the other side in the position for the Glide. Turn the pack face up and show the bottom card and draw attention to its value. Turn the pack face down again and with the fingertips of the right hand placed under the face of the pack draw off the bottom card and place it aside *face down.*

Turn the pack over again showing the next card and again draw attention to its value. Turn the pack face down again and once again you *apparently* draw the card off the bottom of the pack. Apparently is the operative word in this case. In fact you perform The Glide which means that the card you place aside with the first card is actually the Selected Card.

There are now two cards *face down* on the table, one of which is the Selected Card. You have next to place a third card aside with the first two. Instead of turning the pack face up again, which would expose the fact that you still have the second card on the bottom of the pack, simply perform The Glide and draw off the next card and turn this card *face up* before placing it alongside the first two cards.

The position now is that you have three cards on the table, two face down, and one face up and the centre card is the Selected Card.

Ask the spectator if any one of the three cards was the card he selected. Due to the fact that he saw three cards taken from the bottom of the pack, none of them being the Selected Card, he will naturally answer "no".

Ask him then to point to one of the three cards on the table. If he points to the centre one simply turn it over and reveal that it is the Selected Card. If he points to one of the other cards, pick it up and place it aside. Ask him to point to one of the remaining two cards. Again if he points to the Selected Card turn it over. But if he points to the other card place it aside and explain that from three cards placed on the table he has discarded two and left one sitting on the table. Ask him to name the selected card and, when he does so, ask him to turn the card over on the table. It is, of course, the Selected Card.

THE CARD STAB
To Prepare

The Card Stab is one of the most spectacular of all card effects. Many methods have been devised for achieving this effect but the one we recommend here is one of the simplest. You will need a prepared card. Take two picture cards exactly alike and cut the white border away from one of them on the picture side of the card leaving the centre piece only. Paste this centre piece on to the face of the other picture card and leave it to dry. Once it is dry the card will look exactly the same as before even at a very short distance. Place this card on the bottom of the pack.

To Present

Have a card selected and while the spectator is looking at the card place the pack on the table. Ask him to place his card on top of the pack, then cut the cards and complete the cut. This will place the Selected Card somewhere near the centre of the pack with the special card on top of it.

Now take a piece of newspaper about six inches square and place the pack in the centre of the paper and wrap it up like a little parcel. At this stage point out that the card is somewhere in the centre of the pack and that no one could possibly know its exact position.

Hold the pack in the left hand so that one edge of the pack is upwards, and place the point of a ball point pen on it. If you run the point of the pen along the paper you will suddenly feel it sink into the paper a little as if there is a gap there. In fact there will be a slight gap due to the double thickness at the centre of the special card. If you now push the point of the pen into the paper it will naturally be inserted into this slight gap. Push the pen all the way into the gap until it pierces the paper at the other side of the pack.

You now have the pack wrapped up in paper with the pen piercing both the paper and the pack. Ask the spectator to name the Selected Card. When he does so, split the pack into two halves, by forcing the pen to one side tearing the paper in the process. Having done so, the top card of the *bottom half* of the deck will be the Selected Card.

You may find it necessary to practise inserting the point of the pen into the pack a few times to get the feel of it, but you will find the result is well worth the little practice required.

A CARD TRICK WITHOUT CARDS

An odd title you will say to yourself. How is it possible to do a card trick without cards. Read on. Ask someone just to think of a card. When he has done so, ask him to multiply the value of the card by ten. The Jacks, Queens and Kings, are counted as eleven, twelve and thirteen respectively for multiplication purposes. The Ace has a value of one.

Once he has complied with your request, ask him to multiply the number he now has in his mind by three. Once this has been done tell him:

> If the card was a Club add one to the total he has in mind.
> If the card was a Heart add two to the total he has in mind.
> If the card was a Spade add three to the total he has in mind.
> If the card was a Diamond add four to the total he has in mind.

Now ask him to double the number he is thinking of. If you now ask the person to tell you the number he is thinking of you can immediately tell him the card he has in mind. To make this a little clearer to you we will assume that the spectator has thought of the Eight of Spades.

$$8 \times 10 = 80$$
$$80 \times 3 = 240$$
$$240 + 3 \text{ (for spades)} = 243$$
$$243 \times 2 = 486$$

It is possible to tell that the spectator has

been thinking of the Eight of Spades as soon as he tells you that his total is 486 by adopting the following procedure.

$486 \div 2 = 243$. The last digit which in this case is a three tells you that the card was a Spade. Remember you asked him to add three if it was a Spade. The first two digits which in this case are 24 are divided by three which in this case is eight. Therefore the spectator must be thinking of the Eight of Spades.

Let us take another example. The Two of Hearts.

$2 \times 10 = 20$
$20 \times 3 = 60$
$60 + 2 \text{ (for hearts)} = 62$
$62 \times 2 = 124$

The total which in this instance is 124 is immediately divided by two which gives us 62. The last digit which is a 2 tells us it is a Heart and the first digit divided by three gives us a two. The card is the Two of Hearts.

Remember, when the spectator tells you his total, you immediately halve it. Of the number that is left, whether it has two or three digits the last digit gives you the suit, and the first, or first two digits, divided by three will give the card's value.

THE FOUR ACE TRICK

The title alone — The Four Ace Trick — has become a classic in card magic. Of all the themes that are possible in card magic the Four Ace theme is the one that has possibly intrigued magicians more than any other. There must, by now, be more than a thousand different card tricks in which the Four Aces play an important role. The one we have selected for you is one in which the spectators participate.

To Prepare

For this effect, place the Four Aces on the top of the pack. No one should know that they are there.

To Present

Place the pack on the table and ask someone to cut the pack into two halves. When this has been done, the Four Aces will be on top of one of the halves. Keep a mental note of which half. Now have another spectator cut the two packets into two equal halves so that you now have four packets. Again keep a note of the packet which contains the Aces.

The position now is that you have four packets with the Aces on top of one of the packets. Bend down so that your eyes are level with the table top and look along the table top at the four packets and say: "They aren't quite equal you know".

Now pick some cards off the top of one packet, *not the Ace packet*, and place them on one of the other packets. Look again at them as if it isn't quite right and replace one of the cards on its original packet.

Look at them again and lift two of the Aces from their packet and place them on one of the other packets. You now have two packets with two Aces on top of each.

Look the packets over and say: "No, it's not quite right yet". Now from the two packets that contain the Aces, transfer one card to the other two packets so that you now have an Ace sitting on top of each of the four packets.

Again give them another quizzical look and say: "Yes, by George! I think we've got it". Now quickly turn over the top card of each packet one at a time and your audience will be amazed to see the Four Aces sitting one on top of each packet.

THE FOUR ACE TRICK
NUMBER TWO

The Climax to the previous effect is quite surprising to any audience and as you have the Four Aces sitting there right under their eyes it would be a pity not to use them in the following effect. So at this point we come to the Four Ace Trick Number Two.

To Present

Gather up the Four Aces from the preceding effect and lay them out in a row face down on the table. Gather up the rest of the pack and ask someone to give them a good mix up. The spectator having done so, you take the cards from him and start to deal the cards face down on to the backs of the Aces. You deal three cards on top of each Ace.

In fact, you don't actually deal the cards on to the Aces. You proceed as follows. Hold the pack of cards in your left hand as if you are about to deal cards. Push the first card off the pack to your right hand which takes it and as you do so push the next card off the pack and then the third card, so that you now have three cards in the right hand. Place these three cards in the right hand on to the top of the first Ace, the one at the left-hand side of the row of four Aces.

Now push another three cards off the pack into the right hand and place these three cards on the next Ace. Again you push off another three cards and place them on the third Ace.

Now we come to the last three cards, and you will see the reason for not dealing the cards down one at a time. With the left thumb, spread the top three cards off the side of the pack and bring the right hand over and take the top two only with the thumb on top and fingers underneath. As you do so, the left hand

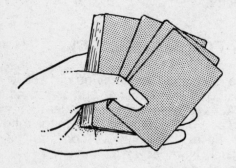

turns so that you can tap the two cards against the top card apparently to square them up. In fact, it is to cover the fact that you have left one of the three cards on top of the pack. Place the two cards you have in the right hand on top of the last Ace and as you do so, you say: "And the last three cards go on top of the last Ace".

The position now is that you have four Aces on the table and three cards are on the top of each Ace with the exception of the last Ace, which only has two cards on top of it, unknown to the spectators of course.

Place the remainder of the packet on the table. Take up the first Ace packet and drop it on top of the deck. Pick up the second Ace packet and drop this one also on top of the deck. Now place the last two packets on top of the others making sure that the Ace which has two cards on top is the last one.

Pick up the whole pack and say: "If I now deal out four cards in a row from left to right, like this (do so), I think you will agree that the last card will be an Ace".

By now you should have four cards on the table. Due to the fact that you only placed two cards on the last Ace, the third card in the row will be the Ace and not the fourth card as the spectators think.

Explain that if you now deal another four cards on top of the first four, you should now have two Aces together in the last packet. Repeat this again with the third set of four cards and still again with the last four cards. The position now is that the spectators think you have four Aces in the last packet when in fact they are in the third packet.

Pick up the first packet and place it into the centre of the pack of cards. This leaves three packets on the table. Pick up the second packet and place this also in the centre of the deck. This leaves two packets on the table, the third packet which contains the Aces and the fourth packet which the audience assumes is the Aces.

Pick up the fourth packet and as you do so, say: "I will place the Four Aces into the centre of the deck. Now watch". Hold the pack in the left hand and with the right fingers riffle the end of the deck. Ask someone to turn over the four cards on the table and lo and behold, the Four Aces.

DO AS I DO
In the Red and Black Card Mystery we introduced a principle of dividing the cards into Red and Black. In "Do As I Do" we utilise a very similar principle with one important difference.

To Prepare
Instead of dividing the cards into Red and Black, we divide them into odd and even cards. That is to say, that one half of the pack

27

consists of all the Aces, (ones), Threes, Fives, Sevens, Nines, Jacks and Kings, and the other half of the pack consists of all the Twos, Fours, Sixes, Eights, Tens and Queens. The Jacks and Kings represent eleven and thirteen respectively and the Queen represents twelve.

Having arranged the pack in this order spread them on the table face up. Without a close study of the cards it would be impossible for anyone to realise that the cards have been arranged in any way. Pick up the cards and spread them faces towards yourself and separate the cards so that you are holding all the odd cards in your left hand and all the even cards in the right hand. Place the two packets of cards on the table face down and ask a spectator to pick up one of the packets. When he has done so pick up the other packet yourself. Now instruct the spectator to do exactly as you do, (hence the title).

Spread the cards with the faces towards yourself. (The spectator repeats your actions.) Pull one card from the centre of the packet and place it face down on the table in front of you. (The spectator repeats your actions again.) At this point pick up the card on the table and look at it and replace it on the table face down and as the spectator repeats your actions say to him; "Now remember the card on the table, don't forget it". Now this is important, although you have asked the spectator to remember the card he has placed on the table, you yourself must completely forget the card you have placed on the table.

Now exchange packets of cards with the spectator. Pick up the card you have placed on the table and place it in the centre of the packet of cards you are holding, and give them a good mix up. (The spectator picks up the card in front of him and inserts it into the packet he is holding and gives his packet a good mix up.) Now exchange packets with the spectator again.

Spread the cards out in a fan, faces towards yourself, and as you do so quickly note the position of the spectator's card. This is quite easy to do because his card will be the only odd card among a packet of even cards, (or vice versa).

Having spotted the card, say to the spectator: "I want you to pull out any card from the middle of the packet like this and place it face down on the table". As you say this you suit the action to the words and pull out the spectator's card and place it face down on the table. (The spectator will pull a card out and place it face down on the table in front of himself.)

At this point ask the spectator to turn his card over. When he does so, look at it in surprise and say, "Good heavens, that's my card! What was your card?" When the spectator names his card, turn over the card and say: "That's funny, you've got my card and I've got yours".

If you study the Do As I Do card trick carefully you will notice that we have introduced still another principle, that of miscalling a card. The card that the spectator places on the table could be any card, but whatever it is, you exclaim that it is your card. The fact that the card that you have placed on the table really is the spectator's card will convince the spectator that the one he has placed on the table really is your card, and there is no reason for him to doubt it.

Tricks With Coins

IT seems there have always been coin tricks, at least since the time that coins first came into circulation. The first book ever to describe how magic tricks were performed, *The Discoverie of Witchcraft*, by Reginald Scot, included several effects with coins.

In recent years there have been a considerable number of magicians who have taken to specialising in coin tricks. The world's leading exponent of coin tricks is probably Al Goshman from California U.S.A. Mr. Goshman can do things with coins that other performers only dream about. He will make them vanish, appear, change from copper to silver and back again, penetrate a solid table top, expand, contract, stretch; you name it he can do it with coins. He uses nothing other than ten fingers and an agile brain.

Another American gentleman, Harvey Rosenthal specialises in effects with coins. Mr. Rosenthal has been responsible for many innovations in coin handling in recent years. Fred Kaps from Holland, is another magician who uses coins consistently in his performances.

The most famous of all coin manipulators was the late T. Nelson Downs from the U.S.A. Mr. Downs travelled all over the world headlining at the largest theatres and performing at private functions for heads of state and crowned heads. Mr. Downs published all of his secrets in a book which has become a much sought after collectors' item.

So, learning a few coin tricks to entertain your friends at a party will put you in good company. Practise all your effects well before attempting to perform them publicly and, when you do so, start with the simpler ones so that you gain a certain amount of performing experience before you graduate to the more difficult items.

HOW TO PALM A COIN

One has often heard the expression, "You must be very good at palming to be a magician". This statement is not one hundred per cent accurate. But there is no doubt that the performer who has, in fact, learnt the basic rudiments of sleight-of-hand, has a great advantage over the man who learns a couple of mechanical type tricks to enable him to appear to be the life and soul of the party.

I don't intend to go into great detail on the many different methods of palming coins, but will confine myself to a few of the most widely used "palms".

First of all the word palm itself is not always strictly correct although most magicians use it to describe practically any method of concealing an object in their hand, whatever position it may be in. There are five basic 'palms' for coins: the classic palm, the thumb palm, the finger palm, the back palm, and the front palm.

THE CLASSIC PALM

There is little more to be said about this 'palm' than the illustration tells you. Note the exact position of the coin in relation to the muscle at the base of the thumb. This muscle presses inwards on the coin, forces it against the fleshy part of the palm and holds it there by applying a slight pressure.

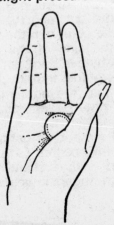

Depending on the actual effect for which you are required to palm a coin, the hand can be held either in a relaxed position or with the five fingers of the hand spreadeagled. This latter can only be achieved after a lengthy spell of practice, and by lengthy we mean several years. But don't despair! You will find that the occasions when you would wish to hold the coin in the Classic Palm position with all five fingers spreadeagled are very rare indeed.

Once you have acquired the knack of holding a coin in this position, try picking another coin up from the table top with a coin in the Classic Palm position. Practise handling other objects with a coin 'palmed'. Holding a coin in the Classic Palm position should become absolutely natural to you. You should be able to hold a coin there while you make all manner of movements with the same hand, such as combing your hair, brushing your teeth or any one of a hundred other actions which are second nature to you already. Only practice will make perfect.

THE THUMB PALM

The Thumb Palm is a misnomer in that the coin is never in the palm at any time. The coin is actually held between the thumb and the base of the forefinger. There are two methods of getting the coin into this position. The first is to hold the coin between the forefinger and thumb. Push the coin with the tip of the forefinger down the side of the thumb until it reaches the fleshy part between the thumb and forefinger where the thumb can now press inwards and hold the coin in position. The forefinger can now be straightened out to its normal position.

The second method of getting a coin into the Thumb Palm position is to hold the coin between the tips of the first and second fingers. Now bend both fingers inwards until the coin

reaches the crotch of the thumb, where it is simply placed in position. Simpler though this second description may be, it requires much more practice than is at first imagined. You should try both methods and use the one which suits your purpose best.

THE FINGER PALM

Once again this is not really a 'palm'. The coin simply rests on the two middle fingers as shown in the illustration. This is a comparatively easy 'palm', perhaps the easiest of all in that it is more or less a normal position in which to hold an object in your hand.

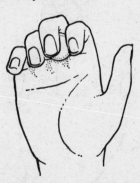

THE FRONT PALM

The illustration shows a coin in the same position as before only this time it is at the front of the hand. If you can master the sleight of transferring the coin continuously from the front to the back of the hand and back again to the front, you can say you are well on the way to becoming a coin manipulator.

THE BACK PALM

The illustration shows a coin held at the back of the hand between the forefinger and little finger. The times when you will require this palm are infinitesimal, but I have included it here for a reason, which I will explain in a moment.

PIVOTING

The illustration shows exactly how the coin is made to pivot back and forth as the two middle fingers push it first one way then the other, travelling from one side of the coin to the other. This continual transfer of a coin from one side of the hand to the other is known as the 'Back and Front Palm'. It will develop a delicacy of touch which is required for all coin work and is a recommended series of movements to be practised constantly. These will develop your sense of touch and control of your fingers in a way that no other movements will. You will find that you are holding the coin so lightly between the first and little fingers that it seems incredible that you don't drop the coin as soon as it starts to revolve.

THE STEEPLE JACK

Another series of movements which will make the fingers supple is the Steeple Jack also known as the Coin Roll. The coin is made to roll over the backs of the fingers in an amazing manner. Once the coin reaches the space between the third and fourth fingers, the thumb reaches under and over to catch it as it slips between the third and fourth fingers, carries it back and pushes it over the side of the forefinger to start it on its way again. When

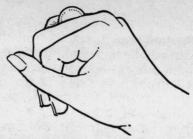

you first start practising the Steeple Jack you
will think it is impossible. It isn't. Some
experts can do it with both hands at the same
time and can make the coins roll first in one
direction then the other.

THE NEST OF BOXES
The Effect
This is one of the most baffling effects in the
realm of close up magic. A borrowed, marked
coin is made to disappear. On the spectator
enquiring where his coin has gone, the
performer replies by reaching into his jacket
pocket and bringing forth a small cardboard
box. He hands the box to the spectator and
asks him to examine it.

On examination the spectator finds that the
box has several rubber bands wrapped around
it tightly. He is asked to remove the rubber
bands and open the box. When he does so he
finds that the box contains another, smaller
box, similarly swathed in rubber bands. He is
asked to open this box. When he does this, he
finds that it contains still another, smaller box,
also wrapped in rubber bands.

On opening this last box he finds a small
cloth bag with one rubber band wrapped
many times around its mouth. On removing
this rubber band he finds within the bag, his
coin, and it is exactly the same coin, not a
duplicate.

You have probably realised that almost any
one of the coin vanishes we have already

explained could be used in this effect. This is true, but there is still another coin vanish which is particularly suitable. A small coin such as a penny is best used for this effect.

To Prepare

You must sew a penny into the hem of a pocket handkerchief.

The problem now is the reproduction of the coin, which, in this instance, has to appear in the middle of the nest of boxes. You will require three boxes which will fit one inside the other. These can be made of wood, metal, or cardboard. The easiest to acquire would be cardboard. In fact, three matchboxes of different sizes would be ideal. You will also need a small cloth bag and last, but certainly not least, a metal or plastic tube through which a coin can slide. This last object, is in fact, called a coin slide.

You commence by slipping the bag over the end of the coin slide and securing it in position with a rubber band wound around it several times. The bag is then placed into the first, or the smallest box and the box closed, leaving the open end of the coin slide projecting out of the box into the air. This box is now swathed in rubber bands which will help to keep the drawer closed and hold the coin slide firmly in position. This box is now placed into the next size box which is closed and wrapped in rubber bands and this box in turn is placed into the third and last box which also has rubber bands wrapped firmly around it.

The finished article should now look like one box with a metal tube projecting from it. If you now drop a coin into the top of the tube it will slide down the tube and come to rest in the little cloth bag. The coin slide can now be withdrawn from the box and the little cloth bag will be left deposited inside the smallest, and innermost of the three boxes.

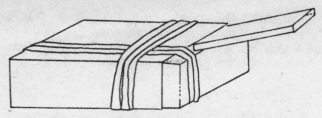

To get at the coin, all the rubber bands will have to be undone and each box opened before you finally get to the little cloth bag and finally the coin.

To Present

Borrow a penny, and have someone mark the coin in such a way that he can positively identify the same coin at a later stage.

While he is marking the coin, remove the handkerchief from your pocket and hold it at its centre so that all four corners are hanging down, with the corner containing the duplicate coin nearest to your body. Take the marked coin in your right hand and place it upwards into the centre of the handkerchief which is of course held in your left hand. As the coin is about to disappear under the handkerchief, the right fingers take hold of the corner of the handkerchief containing the duplicate coin and place the duplicate coin upwards into the centre of the handkerchief where it is held by the left fingers *through the material*. The right hand drops to your side.

A spectator is now asked to hold the coin through the handkerchief. When the spectator holds the coin he has no idea that he is holding a duplicate coin which is actually sewn into the handkerchief.

If you now take hold of one corner of the handkerchief and ask the spectator to release his hold on the coin, you can flick the handkerchief into the air and catch it again as it falls, and, as nothing falls to the floor, the assumption will be that the coin has vanished.

The coin at this moment, is actually held in the performer's right hand.

He immediately reaches into his jacket pocket, in which he has previously placed the nest of boxes, drops the coin into the top of the coin slide, pulls the slide out of the boxes, drops the slide in the pocket and brings forth the nest of boxes, which he immediately hands to a spectator. The spectator takes off the rubber bands, opens the boxes and finally the bag. The coin is then handed to the spectator, who originally marked it, to verify that it is really the same coin.

The illustration helps explain the whole set up. You will find sometimes that the marking of the coin will present a slight problem. There are several ways, for instance asking the spectator to scratch his initials with the point of a nail file, or penknife.

If you intend to perform this effect regularly, it is suggested that you purchase from your nearest stationers a supply of self-adhesive labels which come in all sizes down to a quarter of an inch diameter. One of these can be applied to the coin and the spectator can write his initials on it with a pen or pencil. This is by far the best method because the initials can be checked immediately and easily, without anyone having to peer at the coin to find the scratch marks, which are sometimes quite difficult to read under certain lighting. Take the trouble to make up this effect; it is definitely one of the best.

TO SPIN A COIN WITHOUT TOUCHING IT

The effect of this trick is that you hold a coin on the table, standing up on its edge, with your forefinger. The other forefinger is placed on the back of the first finger and rubbed back and forth along the length of the finger, suddenly the coin which was being held by the first finger starts spinning across the table top.

The secret is very simple. Study the illustration carefully. The coin is held by the left forefinger. The right forefinger is drawn back and forth along the back of the left forefinger.

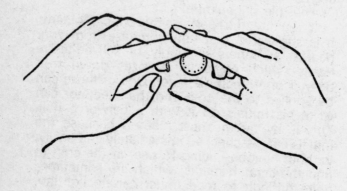

Note the position of the tip of the right thumb. If the right forefinger is drawn right off the end of the left forefinger, the tip of the right thumb will strike the coin and start it spinning across the table top. The coin should be held lightly by the left forefinger to allow the coin to spin. If it is held too firmly and pressure is applied by the left forefinger, all that will happen when the tip of the right thumb strikes the coin is that the coin will fall over.

HEADS OR TAILS

The object of this exercise is to have a person toss a coin on to the table top or floor while you are standing with your back to him and as soon as the coin settles, you immediately tell him whether it is a head or a tail. This can be repeated as often as desired and you will always be correct.

This can be done with practically any round coin. A small notch must be made in the coin, on the edge. This has to be a very small notch in order not to be noticeable. When a coin is tossed into the air and lands on a table top. it doesn't stop as soon as it makes contact with the table, it usually bounces once or twice and then 'settles' gradually on to the table top.

Any coin with a little notch in it will make a different sound on the side with the notch. Try it a few times, first one side then the other. The difference between one side and the other is quite distinct when you are listening for it. You will have to prepare a new coin every time you are going to perform this effect. This is due to the fact that if you carry a coin around for a while in your pocket alongside other change the chances are that the small notch will be rubbed off making the coin unusable for this effect.

THE DISSOLVING COIN

To Prepare

A coin, dropped into a glass of water vanishes completely. A glass disc exactly the same diameter as the coin you intend to use is needed for this effect.

To Present

A coin is placed on the table and can be examined if desired. A handkerchief is held by its centre and the coin is placed under the handkerchief and held by a spectator.

You will realise by now that a substitution has taken place. The glass disc is held in the right hand unknown to the spectators, and as the coin is placed under the handkerchief the glass disc is the one that the spectator holds.

A glass of water is now placed on the table and the spectator is asked to hold the coin over the glass of water. When he does this, the folds of the handkerchief will fall naturally around the glass hiding it from view. Ask the spectator to release his hold on the 'coin' and when he does so the disc will fall into the glass of water with a splashing sound which adds to the effect; the spectators know that the coin has dropped into the glass because they heard it, didn't they? When the handkerchief is removed from the glass the disc cannot be seen as it lies at the bottom of the glass of water.

THE IMPROMPTU DISSOLVING COIN

This is an impromptu version of the Dissolving Coin. There are some performers who think that this impromptu version is far superior to the original version. The effect is similar to the last trick, but without the use of the glass disc.

To Present

A coin is placed under the handkerchief and held by the performer in his right hand. A spectator is now asked to place a glass of water on the performer's left hand. When this has been done, the performer holds the handkerchief over the glass and releases his hold on the coin, which apparently drops into the glass.

In fact the performer tilts the glass slightly so that the coin strikes the side of the glass and lands in the left palm. It is a simple matter under cover of the handkerchief to slip the coin under the glass on to the left palm (see picture opposite).

To prove the coin is really in the glass you remove the handkerchief and allow the spectators to look down into the glass where they can see the coin resting on the bottom of the glass. They can see the coin of course, but what they are unaware of is that the coin is actually under the glass. The water in the glass helps this illusion.

Having proved that the coin is in the glass the performer now places the handkerchief

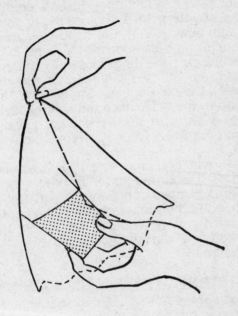

over the glass again. Taking hold of the glass through the handkerchief he lifts it off the left palm which closes immediately to conceal the fact that it is holding the coin, and places the glass still covered with the handkerchief on the table top. He now asks a spectator to remove the handkerchief from the glass and of course the coin is no longer there.

A half pint tumbler will be found to be about the right size and do not have too much water in it. This will prevent you from tipping the glass far enough to allow the passage of the coin.

THE BARE HAND VANISH

As the title implies, this is the complete vanish of a coin in the bare hand. Take a coin, a small coin — *it has to be a small coin* — and hold it against the back of your middle finger-nail. If the coin is smaller than the dimensions of your finger, it is the correct size.

Secretly place a small piece of wax on the nail of your middle finger. Place a coin in the centre of your palm and close the fingers over the coin slowly. Turn the hand over so that it is back up and as soon as the hand is in this position, curl the fingertips into the palm a little tighter and you will find that you are able to press the coin against the back of the nail and on to the wax. Once the coin has adhered to the wax, turn the hand over quickly and open it out fully. The coin will be hidden from view.

You will find that you have to open the hand as it is turning over to prevent anyone getting a glimpse of the coin. If you now close the hand in the same fashion, you can pull the coin off the wax with the aid of your thumb. You can now turn the hand over and the coin has returned.

AN IMPROMPTU COIN VANISH

Apart from pure sleight of hand there are not too many coin vanishes which are of an impromptu nature and can be performed almost at the drop of a hat. In this particular effect a coin vanishes mysteriously from within the folds of a pocket handkerchief. This effect is pure bluff, in that the coin never leaves the folds of the handkerchief, it only 'appears' to have 'vanished'.

To Prepare

Lay a pocket handkerchief out flat on the table and place a coin at its centre. Fold the handkerchief over diagonally until one corner A reaches B. Now fold corner C over until it rests on corner D. The coin remains in exactly the same position throughout this whole procedure. The handkerchief is now rolled up as in the illustration.

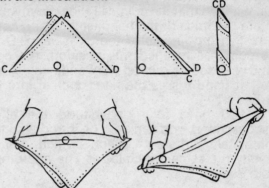

To Present

A spectator is invited to hold the coin through the folds of the handkerchief. The performer now takes hold of the corners C and D and instructs the spectator to release his hold on the coin on the count of three. On the count of three, the spectator releases his hold on the coin and the performer separates his hands quickly keeping a firm grip on the corners of the handkerchief. Once the performer has separated his hands as far as is possible, while still retaining his grip on the corners of the handkerchief, it will seem that the coin is no longer there.

You will have to try this effect first to appreciate this fact. When pulling the handkerchief by the two corners, you open out the handkerchief and it looks empty. The coin is still within the folds of the handkerchief trapped and prevented from falling by the fact that you are drawing it taut between your two hands.

You can if you wish, gather up the handkerchief between your two hands and place it in your pocket with the coin still concealed within its folds, but this is a little unsatisfactory. The following is a much better ploy.

Hold the handkerchief between the two hands and tip the hands so that the left hand is raised a little and the right hand lowered a little. You will find that the coin will slide downwards within the folds of the handkerchief and come to rest in the fingers of the right hand. Once the coin has reached this position, the right hand releases its grip on the handkerchief and the left hand tosses the handkerchief into the air.

If you have fully understood the effect just described, you can now be introduced to a completely different effect, which utilises exactly the same principles as The Impromptu Coin Vanish.

SNEAK IT OUT

A glass is placed mouth downwards on the table top and resting on two coins, with a third smaller coin under the glass. The problem is to remove the smaller coin from under the glass, without touching it with the hands or any other object or by blowing.

The secret of this stunt is to scratch the table cloth in front of the glass continuously.

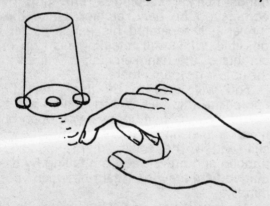

The coin will gradually work its way out from under the glass. This is the reason for the centre coin being smaller, to enable it to travel under the rim of the glass.

SNAP A COIN

Place a small coin on someone's wrist and ask if he can make the coin turn over on his wrist without shaking the coin upwards and without touching the coin with the other hand. After he has pondered for a while, show him how to do it. Place the coin on your own wrist. All you have to do now is snap your finger and thumb together and the coin will turn over. It will need a little practice to do it without dropping the coin on the floor because there is a tendency for the coin to slip off the wrist.

X-RAY EYES

Ask someone to place a coin under a cup, which is placed mouth downwards on the table, while you are out of the room. After he has done this he is to call you to re-enter the room. As soon as you do this, you immediately tell him the value of the coin he has placed under the cup. This can be repeated several times if desired.

The method is quite simple, but you do need a friend to help you, or to use the correct term, a confederate. This friend is appointed to supervise the proceedings. Someone is to place a coin, any coin on the table while you are out of the room and your friend places the cup over the coin. When he does this he arranges the cup in such a way that it signals to you, as soon as you look at the cup, the value of the coin.

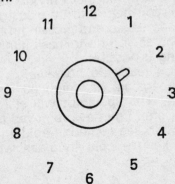

If you imagine the cup to be a clock dial, and the handle of the cup to be a hand pointing to different hours. You can work out your own code, such as one o'clock one penny, two o'clock a nickel , and so on, but always make one of the numbers denote a foreign coin. When this happens, and it will, you can explain that you cannot tell the exact value of the coin because it is a foreign currency. Also make sure that one of the chosen numbers denotes that there is no coin under the cup. There is always one Smart Alec at every party who will pretend to place a coin. In this case your confederate simply arranges the handle accordingly.

This type of effect should not be dismissed lightly because it often has a lasting effect long after the event .

BETCHA CAN'T

This is one of those items where you do something then ask a spectator to repeat your actions. When he does so and thinks he is succeeding, everyone present knows that he isn't. When he realises he has been 'had' it all adds to the fun of the thing.

Place a coin against the centre of your forehead and press it firmly into place where it stays. Keep it there for a few moments while you ask your friends if they think they can duplicate your feat. There is always someone in every gathering who is prepared to have a go, so let him. In fact not only do you let him have a go, you help him by placing the coin against his forehead and pressing it firmly into position and as you do this ask him to keep it there as long as possible.

What you really do however, is press the coin firmly against his forehead and take it away again. The spectator will still 'feel' the coin there, after you have removed it and it is quite funny to see someone holding his head steady to keep a coin in place which isn't there.

HOW TO VANISH FOUR COINS FROM A GLASS

The effect of this 'vanish' on a spectator is as follows. The performer places four coins into a glass for all to see. He shakes the glass and the audience can both see and hear the coins rattling about in the glass. The performer then places a pocket handkerchief over the top of the glass, and secures the handkerchief in place, by means of a rubber band which is placed around the top of the glass and over the handkerchief. After pointing out that it should now be impossible for anyone to remove the coins from the glass, he gives the glass one more shake to assure everyone that the coins are still within the glass and handkerchief. Holding the glass in the left hand, he takes hold of the handkerchief, pulls it off the glass and to everyone's amazement, the glass is empty, the coins have indeed been removed from the glass right under their very noses.

To Present

If you study the illustrations you will see immediately how the effect is achieved. After the coins have been placed in the glass and the handkerchief and rubber band are in position, the glass is given one more shake "to assure everyone that the coins are still there". This is not strictly true. You have another, ulterior motive for giving the glass just one more shake. You will find that with just a little practice, it is possible to shake the coins upwards and over the edge of the glass so that they are held in the handkerchief, and prevented from falling downwards by the rubber band. This can be done in one quick shake. It will help considerably if the handkerchief has not been drawn too tightly over the top of the glass. Once the coins are in this position, the glass can be handled quite freely and can even be placed on the table provided you keep the side of the glass where the coins are hanging away from the spectators.

Hold the glass at the bottom in the left

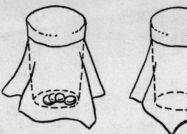
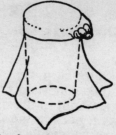

hand, and with the right hand reach up and take hold of the coins, through the thickness of the handkerchief and pull upwards away from the glass. The spectators will see that the glass is now empty, the coins have gone. Although this is technically a simple effect to perform it does require a certain amount of practice to enable you to shake the coins over the top of the glass every time. One thing that must not happen is for three coins to fly up and over and leave one behind. When this happens the least movement of the glass afterwards will betray the fact there is only one coin in the glass.

An alternative presentation for this effect is to have four duplicate coins concealed in the left hand. Place the glass on the left hand on top of the concealed coins. Give the glass a shake to place the coins over the rim of the glass, then lift the glass off the left palm to show that the coins have been shaken through the bottom of the glass, then as an after-thought lift the handkerchief from the top of the glass showing that it is empty.

JUGGLING WITH COINS

Place a stack of coins on your right elbow as in the illustration, and balance them there for a few seconds to allow everyone to see them. The right hand should be held in the position shown, hand cupped, fingers pointing towards the elbow. The problem is to grab the coins in the right hand. This is done by dropping the right elbow downwards suddenly.

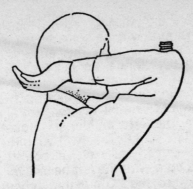

The coins will be left in mid-air for a fraction of a second at which point the right hand travels forward and downwards and catches the coins before they fall. When you first attempt this, use one coin only. Once you have mastered the catching of one coin, add another then another and so on until you can stack up a dozen or more coins and catch them with ease.

The next juggling feat with coins is more difficult but still worth trying. Place two coins on the back of the right hand about four or five inches apart. Raise the right hand quickly

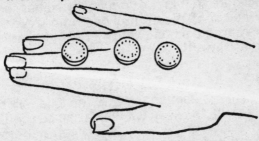

projecting the coins upwards into the air. As the coins fall, you have to catch them one at a time. With two coins it isn't too difficult but to make the effect look really impressive, do it with three coins. Several expert jugglers can catch four, but so far it appears that there have been only three men in the world who could catch five coins one after the other with certainty every time.

In projecting the coins into the air, it will help considerably if the coin nearest the finger-tips is tossed highest. This ensures that this coin will take longer to fall thus giving you more time to catch the others.

Try tossing a coin by flicking it with the thumb in the normal fashion, from the right hand over the left shoulder and down into the waiting left hand. This will require a lot of practice. Once you have mastered this, try tossing a coin with the left hand over the right shoulder into the right hand. If you can do either of these it shouldn't take you too long to master tossing two coins, one from each hand, over the opposing shoulders and catching both coins one in each hand.

The toe and knee catch should not be too difficult for football players. Place a coin on the right toe and toss it up gently and catch it on the right knee. From the right knee toss it up and over to the left knee. This is similar to a football player's exercise. From the left knee toss it down on to the tip of the left toe. Once you have reached this stage, reverse the whole procedure so that the coin finally comes to rest on the tip of the right shoe. From there, kick it up into the air and catch it in your hand as it falls earthwards

THE BALANCED COIN

This little item comes into the category of a party stunt, the knack of which can be acquired with a few practice trials. Having performed it, you can now sit back and watch your friends try to duplicate your feat. Some of them will in fact succeed and when this happens, it will make the others try a little harder.

To perform The Balanced Coin place a thin piece of card, a playing card is ideal, on your fingertip and balance it there. Now place a coin on top of the playing card, so that it is exactly over the fingertips. The picture

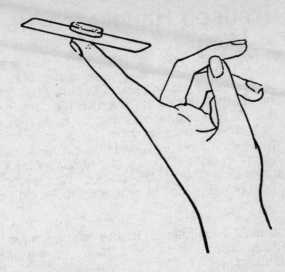

illustrates this perfectly. The problem is to remove the card and leave the coin balanced on the fingertip. The edge of the card is flicked with the back of the middle finger, the card flies through the air and the coin stays exactly where it is on the tip of the finger.

With practice you will be able to perform this but to enable you to do so quickly, we suggest you resort to the following method. Neither the card nor coin is balanced exactly on the tip of the finger but more on that part of the finger which contains the finger-print. To do this, it simply means that instead of holding the finger upright, tilt it a little away from you.

Transpo Handkerchiefs

The Effect

The performer wraps a red chiffon handkerchief in a piece of newspaper and places it on one side of his table. It is important at this point that he draws attention to the fact that it is a RED handkerchief that he is wrapping in the newspaper. He now picks up a blue chiffon handkerchief and wraps this one similarly in another piece of newspaper, again emphasising the BLUE colour. This second handkerchief is placed on the opposite side of his table.

"Now," says the performer, "a miracle is about to take place. On the left we have a red handkerchief, on the right we have a blue handkerchief. I merely command them to change over and they obey me so quickly that it is impossible to see them pass."

At this point he picks up the paper which apparently contained the red handkerchief, tears it open and shows that it now contains the blue one, then picking up the other paper shows that this now contains the red one.

To Prepare

You will require four handkerchiefs of thin chiffon or silk, two red and two blue, plus two prepared pieces of newspaper. The papers are prepared by placing one piece of newspaper on the table and placing one red handkerchief in the centre. A second piece of newspaper is now pasted around the edges and placed on top of the first piece, over the handkerchief and pressed down firmly around the edges. You now have a double piece of newspaper with a red handkerchief concealed in the centre.

Two other pieces of newspaper are prepared in exactly the same way with a blue handkerchief concealed within the double thickness. The prepared paper containing the blue handkerchief is placed on the left of your table and the paper with the red handkerchief is placed on the right. The remaining two handkerchiefs are lying on the table in full view.

54

To Perform

The red handkerchief is picked up and wrapped in the paper containing the blue handkerchief and placed on the left of the table. The blue handkerchief is wrapped in the other paper (containing the red handkerchief) and placed on the right of the table. After the performer has commanded the handkerchiefs to change places, it is now a simple matter to pick up the paper on the left and tear through the thickness of the *outer paper* to show the blue handkerchief. A similar treatment to the other paper will show that it now contains the red handkerchief. Care must be taken when tearing the paper that *only the outer thickness* of the paper is torn, to avoid exposing the fact that there is another handkerchief contained within.

The Transpo Handkerchief effect should never be performed with lights behind you, because a strong light shining on the back of the paper will show the outline of the concealed handkerchief. The same rule also applies to performing in daylight with the sun behind you, or in front of a window.

The Broken Match Restored

The Effect

A plain, ordinary, everyday matchstick is placed in the centre of a pocket handkerchief. The handkerchief is now wrapped around the matchstick and a spectator is invited to feel the matchstick through the folds of the handkerchief to make sure that it is still there. Once the spectator has verified this fact, he is asked to break the matchstick in two through the folds of the handkerchief. The handkerchief is now slowly and deliberately unfolded, and there, lying in the centre of the handkerchief, is the matchstick completely restored and in one piece.

To Prepare

The secret is very simple. Beforehand, place a matchstick in the hem of a pocket handkerchief. Push it well into the hem because you might be embarrassed later if it were to fall out.

To Perform

With this matchstick concealed in the hem, lay the handkerchief out flat on the table and place a second matchstick in the centre. Fold the handkerchief in two with the matchstick in the centre. Fold it over a few more times but make sure that you keep track of where the duplicate match is concealed in the hem. Pick up the folded handkerchief and allow the

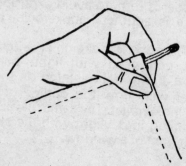

spectator to feel the match through the thickness of the handkerchief. While the spectator is feeling the match, ask him to break it in two. After he has done this it is now a simple matter to unfold the handkerchief and show the whole match.

Balancing a Handkerchief
The Effect

If someone were to ask you if you could balance a handkerchief on your chin or on the tip of your nose, you would probably say it was impossible. But it isn't. It can be done. The handkerchief is prepared by sewing a thin wire into the handkerchief from one corner to the other diagonally. The easiest way to do this is to sew two handkerchiefs together with the wire concealed between the two thicknesses.

To Perform

Hold the handkerchief by two corners with the wire at the corner held by the right hand.

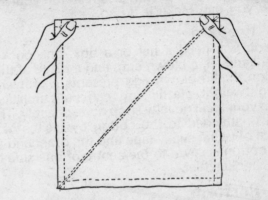

Show the handkerchief on both sides by turning it around. Drop the corner held by the left hand so that the handkerchief is now hanging from the right hand. The left hand now takes hold of the corner hanging right at the bottom and lifts this corner up so that the handkerchief is now held in a horizontal position between the two hands. The handkerchief is drawn taut between the two hands, to disguise the fact that there is a wire sewn into it.

You now spin the handkerchief between the two hands to wrap the loose ends around the wire. Turn the hands so that the handkerchief is now in a perpendicular position. In this position, still held between the two hands, it can be lifted up and placed in position on the chin and balanced.

If a thin copper wire is used, the handkerchief can now be removed from the chin and wrapped around one hand disproving any theories the spectators may have about anything being concealed in the handkerchief.

The Egg Laying Handkerchief

The Effect

Do you believe a handkerchief can lay eggs? Read on and you will discover for yourself how you can make it do so.

To Prepare

You will need a hat or a box, one pocket handkerchief, a blown egg, and a piece of thin cotton. If the blown egg presents a problem, a lightweight plastic egg can be purchased from your local novelty shop quite cheaply. The egg is attached to the cotton by means of a piece of white sticky tape and the other end of the cotton is sewn to the centre of one side of the handkerchief.

To Perform

The hat is already in position on your table with the handkerchief behind it, draped loosely over the egg. First of all the hat is shown to be empty and replaced on the table in front of the handkerchief. The handkerchief is now picked up by two corners, so that the egg will hang down behind the handkerchief. Note that the handkerchief is held taut between the hands and that in this position, the egg is hanging just below the centre of the handkerchief. Wave your hands a little so that the handkerchief will sway in the air, but not too much.

Explain to your audience that the handker-

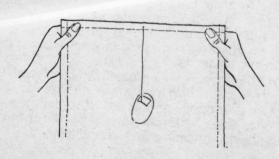

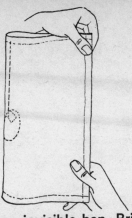

chief contains an invisible hen. Bring the top two corners of the handkerchief together, folding it in half, so that the fold is towards the audience, and take hold of both corners in the left hand. The thumb and fingertips of the right hand slide down the edges of the handkerchief until they reach the two bottom corners, at which point they take a firm grip on both corners. These two corners are now lifted up so that you are now holding the handkerchief with two corners in each hand and the handkerchief forming a sort of closed hammock between.

In this position you can now lift the right hand corners up and the egg will roll out of the fold of the handkerchief. Make sure that you are holding the handkerchief reasonably close to the hat so that the egg will drop into the hat.

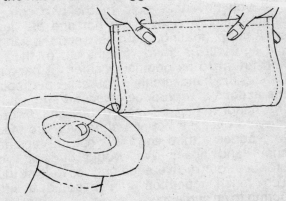

If you hold the handkerchief too high you will find that the egg will be left hanging in mid air on the end of the piece of cotton for all to see.

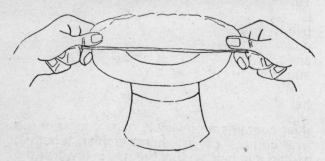

You have now produced one egg, which is now in the hat. Unknown to the audience there is a piece of cotton between the egg and the handkerchief. Release your grip on the handkerchief with the left hand and take the other two corners one in each hand, and open the handkerchief out between them. The bottom edge of the handkerchief should be just above the brim of the hat. You must now drop the handkerchief with a forward throwing motion so that the handkerchief will land with the two bottom corners and edge, across the hat, and the top edge on the table in front of the hat. In doing this, the spectators can see both sides of the handkerchief.

If you now take hold of the two corners which are laying over the hat and lift them straight up, holding it taut between the hands, the egg will be lifted straight out of the hat and return to its original position of hanging behind the handkerchief. You can now repeat the actions and produce a second egg, and if the handkerchief is opened out and thrown forward over the hat as before, you are ready to produce a third egg. This can be repeated again and again. We would suggest you produce four or five eggs and leave it at that. Too much repetition can become a little boring to an audience.

The Shower of Sweets

The Effect

This is more than one hundred years old and is still performed by magicians today. It has been well and truly audience tested and is guaranteed to win friends and influence people, and is particularly suitable for performing to an audience of schoolchildren.

A handkerchief is shown on both sides then held above a plate. The handkerchief is given a shake and a shower of candies fall from within the folds of the handkerchief and fill the plate to almost overflowing.

To Prepare

Four things are required. An ordinary pocket handkerchief, a special holder to hold the candy, a plate, and the candy. Study the illustration carefully to see how the holder is constructed. A square of white linen has two of its corners folded into the centre until they meet. The two edges which meet are sewn together. At the top corner is a sort of double hook which is sewn to the corner of the holder. In this position you will see that the holder is a triangular pocket which hangs upside down with a double hook at the top. The bottom corner has a small ring sewn to it. If the pocket is now filled with sweets and the bottom corner folded up, the ring can be looped over one of the hooks, the lower one in fact. The holder can now be suspended from the upper hook and the candy will be held inside the pocket.

To Perform

The holder already loaded with candy is placed in the right-hand jacket pocket with the upper hook hanging over the lip of the pocket. Pick up the ordinary handkerchief and hold it by two corners and shake it to show that it is nothing more than it appears. Hold the handkerchief in front of and up against your body. Bring both hands towards your jacket pockets so that you are holding the handkerchief as if

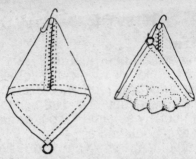

wearing an apron. In this position it is a simple matter to insert the middle finger of the right hand under the hook which is projecting over the lip of the pocket.

Now at this point three things happen almost simultaneously. The left hand releases its grip on the corner of the handkerchief, the right hand lifts the corner it is holding straight up in the air, taking the holder with it, hanging behind the handkerchief, and the performer says: "One pocket handkerchief". You are really secretly stealing the holder from the right-hand pocket and as you do so you say: "One pocket handkerchief" to draw attention to your face and away from the handkerchief for a brief moment.

You are now standing with the handkerchief held by one corner in the right hand with the holder behind it. The left hand picks up a small plate from your table and places it under the handkerchief. The handkerchief is given a slight shake and as you do so the right finger pushes the ring off the lower hook to release the flap which drops and allows the candies to shower downwards on to the plate.

You will find by experimentation that if you give the handkerchief a sharp up and down shake, you can actually dislodge the ring from the lower hook therefore eliminating any need for the fingers of the right hand to lift it. The holder itself should be made from an old linen handkerchief which is of the same texture as the handkerchief from which the production

Stretching a Handkerchief

The Effect

This is a perfect optical illusion and has to be seen to be believed. A gentleman's pocket handkerchief is much larger than one would assume and when you take your measurement from one corner to the other, which is diagonally opposite, it is much longer still. Add to this the fact that there is a certain amount of stretch in linen anyway you will begin to realise that the illusion can be very effective indeed. You will find that it is possible to create the illusion some of the time by merely stretching the material.

To Perform

Take the handkerchief in both hands one at each corner diagonally opposite and twist it rope fashion by twirling it between the hands. As you do so, gather about four inches of each of the two corners into the two hands. Twirl the handkerchief for a few moments, suddenly pull it taut between the two hands and immediately relax a little and start twirling it

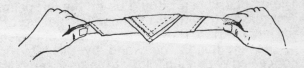

again. After a few moments pull it taut again between the hands for a second and once again relax and continue the twirling motion. Each time the handkerchief is pulled taut you release half an inch or so from each hand so that every time the spectator sees the handkerchief pulled taut it is a little longer than before.

A Production Effect

The Effect

Do not dismiss this immediately as being too simple and basic to fool anyone. Performed at the right moment it can be so effective as to cause true astonishment on the part of a spectator. A handkerchief is draped over the the left palm. The centre of the handkerchief is now lifted by the fingers and thumb of the right hand until the handkerchief is lifted clear of the left palm. The left hand is shown back and front then reaches under the fold of the handkerchief and produces a magic wand. For impromptu performances, a pencil could be substituted for the wand.

To Perform

The wand is concealed in the left sleeve. The handkerchief is draped over the left palm. The right hand reaches over and takes hold of the centre of the handkerchief and at the same time takes hold of the end of the wand. The centre of the handkerchief is now lifted straight up into the air taking the wand with it. The emphasis here should be on the left palm. The reason for lifting the handkerchief up off the left hand is to show that nothing is concealed in the left hand. The wand by this time is concealed within the folds of the handkerchief. It is now a very simple matter to reach upward into the folds of the handkerchief with the left hand and produce the wand.

Needless to say, any other object which can fit into the sleeve can be produced in this manner. The more ludicrous the object, the more effective will be the production. For instance who would expect you to produce a stick of rhubarb from a handkerchief at a party. If you can produce something offbeat and unexpected you will soon gain a reputation which belies the simple means you are utilising.

A Comedy Illusion

The ability to make people smile is one of the greatest gifts a person can have. Some people can do it naturally, others have to work at it, and still others have a stock of impromptu gags and bits of business up their sleeve which can be brought into play at a moment's notice. The following 'illusion' falls into this category.

The Effect

Take your handkerchief and draw the centre up through your fist so the centre of the handkerchief is sticking upwards into the air. You take hold of the handkerchief between the left fingers and thumb, while the right hand apparently pulls a hair from the top of your head. The end of the hair is apparently tied or twisted around the centre of the handkerchief, and when pulled upon, causes the handkerchief to wiggle up and down.

To Perform

The whole presentation of this item is of a zany nature. There is no hair merely a little acting. Proceed as follows. Draw the centre of the handkerchief up through your right fist. Take hold of the handkerchief with the left fingers and thumb. The centre of the hand- kerchief is sticking up in the air. If you are holding the handkerchief correctly, you can

make it wriggle up and down by pushing the left thumb up and down.

Pretend to pull a hair from your head and pretend to twist the end of the hair around the centre of the handkerchief. Holding the other end of the 'hair' you pull on it and the centre of the handkerchief will be pulled down to an angle of forty-five degrees. Apparently relax the pull on the hair and the handkerchief will revert to its original position. This should not be done slowly, but in short sharp jerks which are more amusing.

To bring this little mini-illusion to a climax pull the 'hair' further than normal so that the handkerchief is in an almost horizontal position. Lean forward and 'bite' the 'hair' so that it apparently snaps and the handkerchief pops up quickly to its original position. Gather up the handkerchief and place it back in your pocket.

The Devil's Handkerchief

The Effect

The Devil's Handkerchief is a utility prop which can be used in conjunction with many other magic tricks. Basically it is a handkerchief which will enable you to make small objects disappear.

To Prepare

You require two handkerchiefs which should be cotton and of the fancy coloured pattern type. Both handkerchiefs are sewn together around the hem stopping halfway around two sides. Two rows of stitching are then inserted at the point where the previous stitches have stopped. These travel inwards so that they meet in the centre of the handkerchief. This will leave one corner, or in fact one quarter of the handkerchief double and open around the edges.

To Perform

Open the handkerchief out for all to see then gather all four corners up into one hand so that the handkerchief hangs down forming a bag. Place a coin with the right hand into the centre of the handkerchief, actually placing it into the double section. You can now open out the handkerchief and show that the coin is no longer there. To do this you must ensure that the fingers keep a firm grip *on the double corner* and that this corner is held uppermost.

An alternative method of making the Devil's Handkerchief is to sew both handkerchiefs all

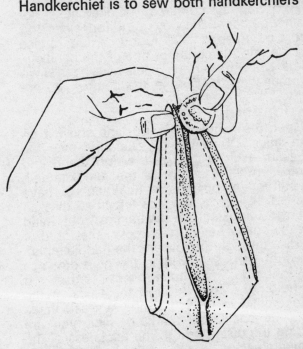

the way round and leave one half of one side open. This second method is recommended if you intend to vanish small objects only. Anything larger than a packet of cigarettes or a bar of chocolate will present a little difficulty in trying to insert them into the opening. You may think that a bulge will show in the handkerchief where the object is concealed. There is a bulge but it will be invisible at even short distances if the handkerchiefs have a brightly coloured jazzy type pattern on the outsides which are seen by the audience.

Another Double Handkerchief

The Effect

This handkerchief is also used for vanishing small objects where it is necessary to keep hold of the object.

To Prepare

Two brightly coloured handkerchiefs are sewn together all the way round four sides, but before doing so, a small round cardboard disc is sewn into the centre of one of the handkerchiefs. Once the handkerchiefs have been sewn together with the disc in the centre, you are ready.

To Perform

Open the handkerchief out and show it on both sides. Drape the handkerchief over the left palm. Hold a coin in the right hand and place it into the centre of the handkerchief, but still retain your grip on it. When you have reached this stage, turn the left hand over so that the handkerchief covers the right hand and the coin. The left hand now takes hold of the disc through the folds of the handkerchief. The right hand still holding the coin drops to the right side. The situation now is that you are holding a coin through the folds of the handkerchief in the left hand. At least, that's what the spectators think. In fact, you are holding the disc, through the thickness of the handkerchief.

The left hand tosses the handkerchief into the air and as it drops downwards the left hand catches it and gives it a shake to show that the coin has vanished. The coin is disposed of in such a way as to make it appear somewhere else, such as the Nest of Boxes trick which is described in 'Tricks With Coins', a chapter on page 36.

Needless to say, you will realise that if the shape in the double handkerchief is different, then other objects can be vanished. For instance, if the shape is that of a playing card, or a box of matches then those would be the objects that would vanish into thin air.

The Cut and Restored Handkerchief

The Effect

This is a beautiful magic trick, which at least one member of your audience will remember long after you have left. Having borrowed a handkerchief from a willing spectator the performer grasps it in his left fist so that the centre of the handkerchief projects above the left fist and the remainder hangs down below the left hand. With a pair of scissors the centre of the handkerchief is cut away from the handkerchief. This piece that has been cut from the centre of the handkerchief is taken in the right hand and pushed under the handkerchief and upwards into the folds of the handkerchief. The handkerchief is now taken from the left hand and shaken. When the handkerchief is opened out fully it is seen that it is undamaged and has become completely restored to its original condition.

To Prepare

All you require for this effect in addition to the handkerchief and a pair of scissors is a paper handkerchief. Cut a piece from the paper handkerchief about three inches square and discard the remainder. This small piece, of which the audience is unaware, is held secretly in the crotch of the left thumb and forefinger.

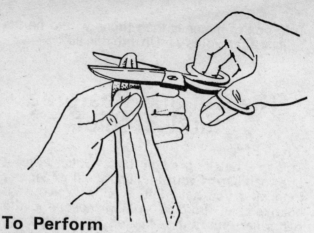

To Perform

Borrow a white handkerchief from a member of the audience. Take the handkerchief by the centre, letting the remainder hang down and place the centre of the handkerchief into the left fist. With the right forefinger and thumb reach into the top of the left fist and pull up the small piece from the paper handkerchief. At this point, hold the left hand over a table and cut the small piece that is projecting above the left fist away, so that it drops on to the table.

The scissors are placed on the table and the small piece of paper handkerchief is picked up in the right hand. This small piece is now placed under the handkerchief and apparently pushed upwards into the fold of the handkerchief. In fact, it is retained in the crotch on the right thumb and forefinger. The right hand is removed from within the folds of the handkerchief, takes hold of one of the corners and pulls it away from the left hand which immediately closes into a fist concealing the piece of paper handkerchief. The right hand remaining gives the handkerchief a shake. The left forefinger and thumb take hold of one of the corners and the handkerchief is opened out to show that it is completely restored.

The handkerchief is now returned to its grateful and probably relieved owner.

The Handkerchief Puppet

This is one way to use up broken dolls. All you require is a pocket handkerchief, an old doll's head and two rubber bands. The head could be from a doll or rabbit, dog or any other old toy. Drape the handkerchief over your right hand and stick the doll's head on the top of your forefinger which should be sticking up under the handkerchief. At this stage it looks like a small puppet with a cloak, but if you wrap two rubber bands over your thumb and middle finger it suddenly looks as if it has hands.

If you have difficulty in obtaining an old doll's head, use a small jam jar, or a ball with a hole in it and paint a face on it.

The Rabbit Puppet

The illustrations will explain this much more clearly than words. The most important point about the Rabbit Puppet, or indeed any form of puppet, is that his effect is improved a hundred fold if he is animated. Make him move like a rabbit. Twist his head from side to side so that the ears will not just be sticking up straight all the time. Make him hop back and forth along the left forearm. Give him a sweet which he can eat and chew on for a few moments before he swallows it.

Talk to him as if he were real and have him behave as if he were human. Say! "Oh! look, he's shy" at which point he is trying to hide behind your forearm or tries to crawl out of sight under your armpit or into your jacket. Have him take a pen or other objects out of your pocket. Scold him and tell him he's a naughty boy. Take the pen and put it back into your pocket, whereupon he immediately steals it again. If you are wearing a wrist watch have him look at the time and pretend he wants to sleep. In short, make him look alive.

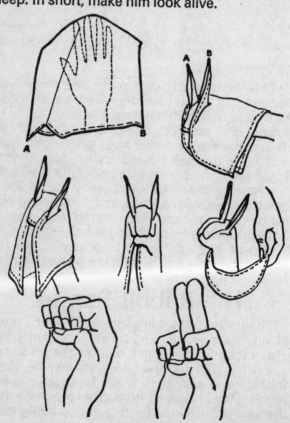

Fatima the Dancer

This is a puppet made from a handkerchief which needs practically no animation whatever in that she will animate herself if she has been constructed properly. Once you have made the puppet, hold the body in the right fingers and the feet in the left fingers. By lifting the body up and down the legs will wiggle a little and the hips can be made to rotate in the fashion of an oriental dancer.

By releasing one of the feet and pulling downwards on the remaining foot and upwards on the body, the other leg will give a high kick and the dancer will spin around.

To Prepare

A glance at the illustrations and you will realise that if you tie a knot halfway along one hem of the handkerchief this will become the head of the dancer. You take hold of the two bottom corners, one in each hand, and roll the handkerchief down towards the knot until it won't go any further. Once the handkerchief is completely rolled up, pull on the two corners stretching the handkerchief slightly, and bring the two hands together and take hold of both corners in the right hand. Take hold of the knot, which is at the bottom, in the left hand, turn the whole thing upside down and you now have Fatima the dancer.

The Magic Mouse

Once again we ask you to study the illustrations carefully to make sure that you understand how the Magic Mouse is constructed. Fig. 19 (page 76) shows the finished Mouse. A tubular body with a tail at one end and a pair of ears at the other. Having made the Mouse, you may ask how it is possible to animate him?

Proceed as follows. Place the Mouse on the left hand, so that he is resting partly on the heel of the palm and partly on the fingertips. Notice that the fingertips are against the rear end of the Mouse under the tail. Bring the right hand over and stroke the back of the mouse from head to tail. As you do so, jerk the tips of the left fingers towards the wrist making the Mouse jump forward an inch or two. Do this a few times and each time the Mouse jumps forward the right hand grabs him and pulls him back to his original position.

Once you have practised this a few times you will find that you can make the Mouse jump five or six inches up the arm. Each time grab him with the right hand and bring him back. To increase the illusion of the Mouse being alive, make him jump a few inches and when the right hand grabs him, instead of bringing him back to his original position, keep a firm grip on him, and 'hop' the Mouse up your left arm before bringing him back to the left hand. You will be amazed at the reaction to this.

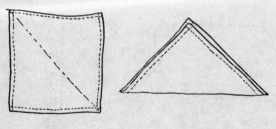

1   2

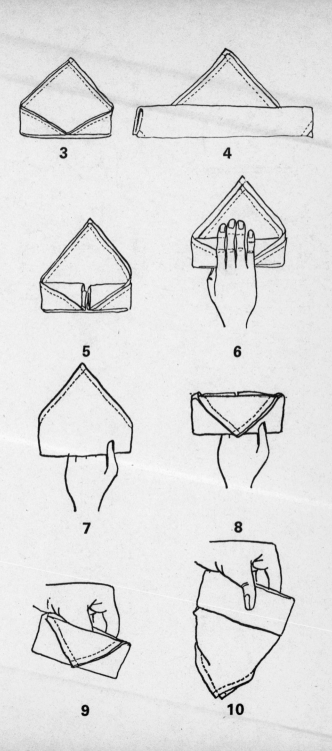

3

4

5

6

7

8

9

10

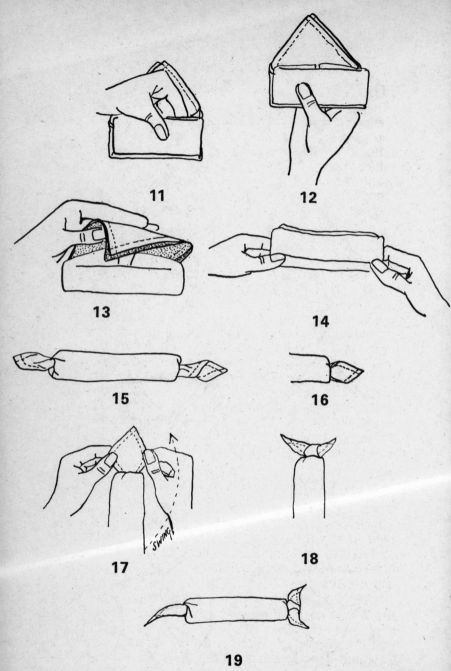

11

12

13

14

15

16

swing

17

18

19

The Knot that will Knot

The Effect

This is another short comedy item which can be performed with a handkerchief and should be used as a prelude to some other stronger effect. You attempt to tie a knot in a handkerchief but no matter how often you try you cannot succeed, despite the fact that the spectators can see that everything is done correctly.

To Perform

Take the handkerchief by one corner of the left hand. The remainder of the handkerchief is hanging down. The right hand takes the bottom corner and brings it up and places it across the top corner which is held between the first two fingers of the left hand. The left thumb holds the second corner across the first. Note that the third and fourth fingers of the left hand are poking through the loop in the handkerchief.

The right hand now reaches through the loop in the handkerchief, turns palm upwards and takes hold of the first corner which was originally topmost, and pulls it through the loop to the right. The handkerchief will straighten out without a knot.

A One-Handed Knot

The Effect

This is a pretty flourish in which a handkerchief held in the right hand is given a shake and tossed into the air and when caught, is seen to have a knot tied in the centre.

To Prepare

Hold the handkerchief over the right hand so that a little more of the handkerchief is hanging over the back of the hand than the front. Note that the portion of handkerchief at the back of the hand leans towards the wrist a little.

To Perform

When ready to perform, the third and fourth fingers curl inwards and take hold of the corner which is over the back of the hand. Let the body of the handkerchief slip over the top of the hand and as it does so, give it a sharp shake down and then up into the air and the knot will appear in the centre of the handkerchief.

The whole effect should be performed with an up and down flourish of the right hand.

A Knotty Problem

The Effect

This is a party stunt which everyone can have a go at before you finally let them in on the secret. Twist a handkerchief rope fashion and lay it on a table parallel to, and a few inches from, the edge of the table. Ask anyone to take hold of the two ends of the handkerchief, one end in each hand and ask them to tie a knot in the centre of the handkerchief without letting go of either end of the handkerchief. Once they have tried and failed, show them how.

To Perform

Fold your arms first. Take hold of the left end of the handkerchief in the right hand and the right end of the handkerchief in the left hand. Now unfold your arms slowly and the knot will form itself.

How to make a Parachute

The Effect

A really excellent parachute can be made from an old pocket handkerchief.

To Prepare

Attach four pieces of string to the four corners of the handkerchief and bring all four ends of the string together and tie a knot about two inches from the ends of the strings. Now tie a heavy washer to the lower ends of the string by passing two of the ends through the washer and tying those two ends to the other two ends. That's it! Simple isn't it?

You will probably have to experiment with several washers to get one of the right weight. If it is too heavy you will find that it will fall to the ground without opening. If it is too light the parachute itself will become distorted in the air and just flutter to the ground, that is if it reaches any height at all.

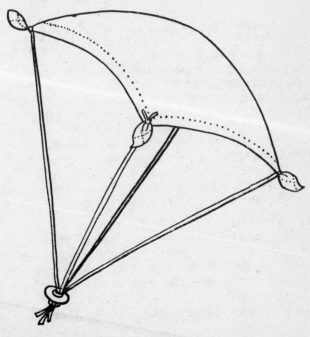

To Perform

Take hold of the handkerchief at the centre, so that the four corners are hanging down with the strings below them with the weight at the bottom. Swing the parachute around gently and throw it upwards into the air. Once it reaches a certain height it will begin to fall and once this happens the parachute will open out and start to float earthwards. Sometimes it will get caught in an updraught and for a while actually float upwards, but eventually it will fall to the ground. You will find that it is better to start off with a light weight and gradually increase it until you have it working properly.

Take Care

The parachute should only be operated in a park or other open place. *Do not stand near anyone* while you are spinning the parachute in preparation to launching it into the air. If the washer should hit someone while you are spinning it, it could be very painful indeed.

The Appearing Knot

The Effect

Removing his handkerchief from his pocket the performer gives it a short sharp shake and a knot appears instantaneously in the lower corner of the handkerchief. That is the effect as the audience sees it. In fact the knot is already in the handkerchief when it is removed from the breast pocket. The knot is tied in one corner of the handkerchief and the handkerchief is held by this corner with the knot concealed by the fingers of the right hand.

To Perform

You will have to practise this to be able to do it successfully every time, but it is not very difficult. As the handkerchief is given a shake the lower corner is shaken upwards so that the fingers can take hold of the lower corner and, at exactly the same moment, the fingers release their grip on the knotted corner. When this corner drops to the bottom the effect of having tied a knot in the handkerchief with one short sharp shake, will have been created.

The Twentieth-Century Handkerchief

Another excellent effect that can be performed with the aid of a Change Bag is the Twentieth-Century Handkerchief Trick.

To Prepare

You will need six handkerchiefs to perform this effect, two red, two white, and two blue. Tie three of the handkerchiefs together in a line by their corners, one red, one white and one blue. Place these three handkerchiefs in one division of the Change Bag, and place the bag on your table. No-one at this point knows that there are three handkerchiefs concealed in the bag. The other three handkerchiefs are lying handy on the table.

To Perform

Pick up the red and blue handkerchiefs which are lying on the table and tie the two of them together with a knot. Show the two handkerchiefs and place them in the Change Bag, on the other side of the partition from the three handkerchiefs. Now pick up the remaining white handkerchief from the table and vanish it by using the Handkerchief Vanisher. Once the handkerchief has gone, pick up the Change Bag and remove the three handkerchiefs tied together. The assumption being that the handkerchief which disappeared is now tied between the other two.

The Magic Camera

THE EFFECT

This is an excellent little novelty, basically a square of paper in the centre of which is a drawing of a camera, the more old-fashioned looking the better. Ask someone to look at the lens of the camera, and smile, because you are going to take his picture with your Magic Camera. Suddenly, while he is looking at the camera and smiling, the camera itself will change to a comical picture of the sitter. The sudden appearance of the picture will be quite surprising and the more comical looking the picture, the better will be the sitter's reaction.

HOW TO MAKE

The "Camera" itself is very simple to make. All you require is a piece of blank paper measuring eight inches by four inches, a felt tipped pen and a small pair of scissors.

DRAW THE CAMERA AND THE COMIC PORTRAIT

Fold the paper in half and on one side of the folded paper make a drawing of a rather old fashioned looking camera. Make sure that the lines are heavy and bold, particularly the lines around the edges of the camera. On the other side of the folded paper, draw a picture frame which is exactly the same size as the camera, again making the outline very bold. Inside this frame make a comical drawing of someone with extra large ears, untidy hair, and other funny features. Should you know in advance that you are going to take a picture of someone with your Magic Camera, be sure to include any of his distinguishing features. If he wears glasses, don't forget to include glasses in the picture. If she's a girl and she wears her hair in a particular style, then exaggerate this style wildly.

CUT ROUND THE CAMERA AND PORTRAIT

Now you have the drawing of the camera on one side of the folded paper and the comical picture on the other side. Take a pair of small sharp scissors and cut around three sides of the camera just inside the outer line. Leave the top side of the camera intact. Now cut around three sides of the comical picture, but this time leave the bottom edge of the square intact. A glance at the picture will give you a threequarter and side view of how the cuts should be made. Lift up the camera cut out and tuck it over the top of the picture. If you now press the two halves of the folded paper together the result will be that the camera will be showing on the side that is shown to the spectator.

PRACTICE YOUR MAGIC IN A MIRROR

At this point in the proceedings we recommend that you stand in front of a mirror to see the effect you are about to present.

Hold the sheet of paper up in front of your body. Hold the rear half of the paper at the

bottom right corner between the forefinger and thumb of the right hand and hold the front half of the paper at the bottom left corner between the forefinger and thumb of the left hand. Now lift up the rear half of the paper quickly with the right hand and suddenly the picture will appear where the camera was. You will see that the camera is lifted up over the comical picture, exposing the picture to view. Once you have lifted up the rear half drop it back down again quickly, to ensure that the flaps stay flat.

The Patriotic Paper Balls

THE EFFECT

The balls referred to in the title of this effect are actually made of tissue paper. Each ball is, in fact, one sheet of tissue paper crushed into a ball. The balls are picked up, one at a time, and placed into the containers so that you have three red balls in one container, three white balls in the second container, and three blue balls in the third container. A magic pass is made and the three containers are turned over and to everyone's amazement, there is a red, a white and a blue ball in each container. The containers are otherwise empty.

TO PREPARE

You will need nine balls altogether, three red, three white and three blue. You will also need three hats or cardboard boxes or similar containers. These containers should be of a size that will enable you to place your hand inside each one easily. The three containers should be sitting in a row on the table with three balls in front of each container, so that there are three red balls in front of one container, three white balls in front of the next container and three blue balls in front of the third container.

TO PERFORM

This is an extremely simple effect and the only other requirement apart from those already listed, is a little bit of sleight of hand. Place the three containers on the table and place three balls in front of each container — three red, three white and three blue. The balls should be nearest to the audience.

Stand at the side of the table facing the table with your right side to the audience. Pick up a red ball in your right hand and place your hand into the first container. As you do this it is natural for your hand to drop out of sight into the container. Once your hand is inside the container, grip the ball in what magicians call the 'finger palm'. Bring your hand (and the red ball) out of the container and immediately pick up the white ball. Put your hand into the second container and, as your hand drops out of sight inside the container, release the red ball and 'finger palm' the white ball. Remove your hand (and the white ball) from the container and pick up a blue ball which is apparently placed into the third container only this time the white ball is deposited into the third container and the blue ball is retained in the 'finger palm'.

WHAT THE SPECTATORS THINK

So while it seems that you have dropped a red ball in the first container, a white ball in the second container and a blue ball in the third container, IN FACT there is no ball in the first, a red ball in the second and a white ball in the third. The blue ball is still concealed in the right 'finger palm'.

CONTINUE THE DECEPTION

Repeat the procedure — pick up a red ball but drop the 'palmed' blue ball into the first container, pick up a blue ball and drop the 'palmed' red ball into the THIRD container, pick up a white ball and drop a 'palmed' blue ball into the SECOND container. The end of the second round leaves you with the white ball 'palmed'.

Now pick up a red ball and drop the 'palmed' white ball AND the red ball into the first container, pick up the white ball and put it into the second container and lastly pick up the remaining blue ball and put it into the third container.

You now have your red, white and blue balls in the three containers. Say the magic words or make a magic pass and show your astounded audience the contents of the containers.

None of these movements are difficult. The tissue balls used should be quite small, say half an inch in diameter, and the trick should be practised with the actual balls you intend to use in the performance.

Timing is all important. Practise the moves so that you can perform them without hesitation. All your actions should be deliberate; any falter in the timing will give the impression that you are not quite sure which ball goes into which container and if this happens it will lead to confusion in the minds of your spectators. The effect should be simple and direct.

The Revolving Snake
HOW TO MAKE
A FASCINATING NOVELTY

First of all mark out the outline of a snake on a sheet of paper as in the illustration. The

paper should be fairly stiff but not too thick. Cut away the surplus paper around the snake and once you have done this start cutting at the point marked and follow the line right through until you reach the centre of the snake. You can now open out the snake so that it forms a spiral.

You now require a length of wire – an old wire coathanger will do – and you must bend it into the shape shown so that it can sit comfortably on top of a table lamp, with one end pointing upwards from the centre. The snake must be carefully balanced on the point of the wire.

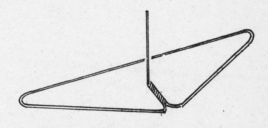

After a few moments the snake will start to spin and it will continue to spin just as long as the lamp is alight. Once the lamp is extinguished, the snake will stop revolving. This is due to the air above the lamp becoming hot, and as this happens the air rises upwards. More air comes in at the bottom of the lampshade and this air in turn become hot and rises, so that in fact there is a continuous current of air travelling upwards causing a slight draught. This is the power that is responsible for the movement of the snake.

You may have to vary the shape of the wire a little according to the shape of the lamp you use, but as long as you understand the principle involved it should be a simple matter to devise your own shape. The revolving snake can make an interesting series of moving shadows on a ceiling or wall due to its position or to the opaqueness of the lampshade used.

An Impromptu Propellor
A PARTY COMPETITION
This is a good stunt for parties in that you can hold a competition to see who can make the propellor revolve for the longest period.

HOW TO MAKE
Take a small piece of tissue paper about the size of a cigarette paper, in fact a cigarette paper is ideal for this experiment. Fold all four sides of the paper up at right angles so as to form a small paper tray as shown below.

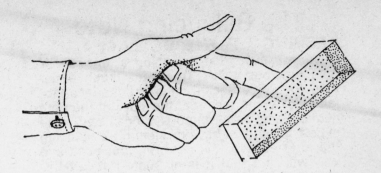

HOW TO OPERATE

Hold this carefully in one hand and place it against the forefinger tip of the other hand. Release your grip on the paper and as you do so start to move the finger forward. If you have placed the forefinger at the centre of the tray, it will start to spin like a propeller almost immediately. To keep it spinning you have to keep it moving and the easiest way to do this is to move your arm around continuously in a circle. After a few moments you will discover at exactly what speed the hand must travel to keep the propellor spinning. If you move too slowly it will drop to the floor, too fast and it will blow away.

The Impromptu Propellor is best tried indoors rather than in the open air. It is also possible to place the tray against the tip of your nose and by walking forward quickly the tray can be made to revolve. One word of warning on this however. The tip of the nose spin should only be attempted in a hall, or gymnasium where there are no obstructions, because once you try it you will realise that your eyes are glued to the tray on the tip of your nose and you will be unable to see where you are going.

The Balancing Note

KEEPING UP THE DOLLAR

Have you ever tried balancing a one dollar note on your nose? Try it, it's much easier than you think. Because it is so light, it cannot fall quickly and the air at the sides of the note actually acts as a support. A crisp new note is best. Once you have mastered it try placing the long edge of the note on your nose and you will find that it is no more difficult this way than it is standing up on end. You can practise by placing the note on your forefinger.

PING-PONG ON THE NOSE

Another similar balancing feat is with a sheet of paper twisted into a cornucopia. The point is placed on the tip of your nose or your forehead and the whole is balanced there. You can add to the interest by tossing up table tennis balls and catching them in the open end of the cornucopia. You will find that it is not too difficult to get the balls in the open end, the difficulty is in keeping the whole thing balanced on the tip of your nose after the balls have landed inside. One little tip. The taller the cornucopia the easier it is to balance, but of course it makes it more difficult to catch the table tennis balls.

The Hindoo Papers

THE EFFECT

A small paper packet is shown and unwrapped. Inside, is another small packet and when this one is unwrapped there is a third paper packet. This third paper is unfolded and shown to be just a piece of paper. Ask for the loan of a one dollar bill and have someone make a note of the number. Take the note and fold it into four and place it in the centre of the third and smallest paper. Re-fold the paper around the note. Place this in the centre of the second paper and re-fold it. Finally place this packet into the largest paper and re-fold. A magic pass is now made and the papers are unfolded, one at a time as before, but when the centre paper is unfolded the one dollar bill is no longer there.

TO PREPARE

You will require FIVE pieces of paper. ONE of the papers should be approximately six inches square; the next TWO papers should be five inches square and the remaining TWO pieces should be three and a half inches square. The best paper to use is a heavy grade which can be folded and creased firmly.

Fold all of the five papers up into small packets, as shown in the illustration, and press down hard on the creases so that when the papers are unfolded they will retain the creases as shown. Take the two middle size

91

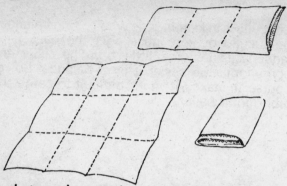

packets and paste them back-to-back so that they will appear as one packet, but, unknown to the spectators it is a packet which can be opened from either side.

Set the papers by folding the two smallest pieces and placing one in each side of the double paper. Fold those papers to look as if they are one packet and place this packet in the centre of the largest paper. Fold this last paper up around it.

TO PERFORM

When you are ready to perform the effect remove the small packet from your pocket and place it on a table in front of you. Proceed to unfold the first paper quite slowly and deliberately and open it out flat on the table. The second packet, which has now been exposed to view, should also be unfolded until the third packet is seen. This third packet should be picked up from the table and unfolded to show that it is nothing more than a piece of paper.

The one dollar bill , when borrowed, should be folded to such a size that it will fit into the centre of the paper. The paper should now be wrapped around the note.

Hold this packet in your right hand and pick up the second paper with your left hand, *being careful to keep your fingers underneath to stop the paper on the other side from unfolding prematurely.* Place the paper containing the note into the centre of the second paper and fold the second paper around the first. Draw attention to the third paper lying on the table and as you do so turn the packet over in your hand. Place the packet into the centre of the third paper and fold the third paper around the second.

All the dirty work has now been done. All you need do now is to impress upon your spectators that they are about to witness a miracle. Unwrap the papers slowly, one at a time, until your audience realises that the note is no longer there. Once the point has been made that the note really has vanished, start re-folding the papers, *making sure that you turn over the second paper as before.*

If someone asks where the note is, tell him that it is still in the centre of the papers. Unfold the papers once more and when you reach the centre paper hand it to the person who loaned you the note and let him unwrap the last paper and of course, when he does so, he will find his note. Ask him to check the number to make sure that it really is the same note. If anyone asks how it works, explain that it is an optical illusion. The note really was in the papers all the time but the creases in the paper gave the illusion that the note was no longer there.

You will realise of course that any small flat object such as a cardboard disc or a coin can be made to disappear in this way. They can also be made to change from one object to another simply by placing another coin or disc in the centre of the other small paper. Incidentally, should you decide to borrow a dollar bill note for use in the above effect then the following effect is a perfect sequel to it.

Folding Money

This is a simple but very effective little novelty with a borrowed bill . Basically you show the note to someone and ask him to watch your hands very carefully as you fold the note to one eighth its size. Without making any false moves whatever, you now unfold the note and somehow, miraculously it has turned upside down. Usually when you perform this effect for someone, he will immediately say, "do that again" and you can, immediately, and the more often you do it the more bewildered the spectator becomes.

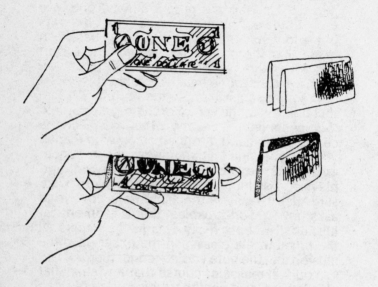

The Paper Tree

A spectacular effect.

TO PREPARE

The Paper Tree is achieved by very simple means. Take a double sheet of newspaper, of tabloid size, and start to roll it into a tube from one side to the other, that is to say across the width of the double page. When it is almost completely rolled up but with a few inches remaining, place another double sheet of newspaper on the end of the first one, as shown below. Now continue the rolling up of the paper so that you have two sheets of newspaper all rolled up in one roll. You can, if you wish, add several other sheets of newspaper to the roll, but remember that the

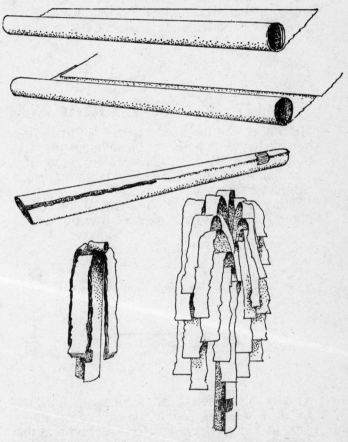

more paper in the roll the taller will be the tree, and if you intend performing this effect indoors, it is more than likely that the ceiling of your house will not be high enough. We suggest that two or three sheets will be enough, at least to begin with.

THE EFFECT

It is advisable, although not exactly necessary, to secure the end of the last sheet with a small dab of paste or a short piece of sticky tape. Once this end of the sheet is secured you must flatten out one end of the roll and tear it down the centre, in two places as shown. Each tear extends down to slightly beyond the halfway mark. Fold back the torn

The Paper Ladder

The Paper Ladder is similar to the Paper Tree in that they both begin in the same manner, i.e. by rolling up several sheets of newspaper into a roll and securing the end with a small piece of sticky tape.

Now start tearing a piece out of the roll as shown. Then fold the ends of the roll over as

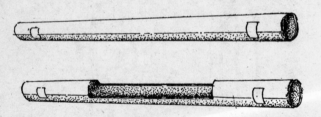

shown and insert both forefingers into the roll, one at either side. In the case of the Paper Tree you lifted upwards. You will find that this is not possible with the ladder. Instead of lifting upwards, you shake downwards and the ladder will drop down to the ground. It will now be possible to lift the ladder up and hold it at the bottom end so that it extends upwards into the air making it appear longer than it really is.

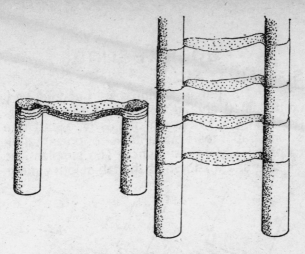

The Garden Fence

The Garden Fence is probably the easiest of all the items in this little paper act. All you require is a sheet of newspaper cut in half and the two ends pasted together to make one long strip of newspaper. Fold this sheet of paper up in accordion pleats, until it is one compact packet. All you need do now is to cut one end of the packet at an angle and open out the whole strip, and you have a Garden Fence.

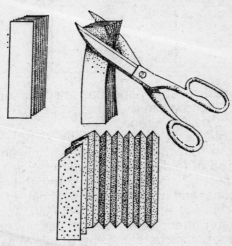

Paper Tearing

SIMPLE TEARS

The art of paper tearing can become very complicated should you decide to go in for presenting a whole act of this type, but one or two paper tears are suitable for presentation to practically any audience. The simplest are those that are known as the tablecloth variety.

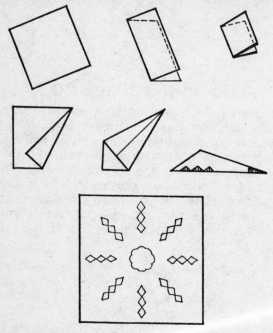

A folded sheet of paper has small sections torn out of it and when the sheet is opened out fully, a pretty design is seen.

A glance at the illustrations will show you how to fold the sheet of paper initially. This method of folding the sheet is the easiest and the best. If you now cut away the shaded portions and open out the sheet of paper you will see the result for yourself. There are probably hundreds of different designs possible the most famous being the Ship's Wheel and the Ring o' Roses.

A variation is to accordion pleat a sheet of paper and cut a design from this and when the sheet is opened out the result will be a long line of either boys, girls, rabbits, monkeys or whatever takes your fancy at that particular moment. If you decide to include this in a performance it is advisable to mark out before hand with a pencil the outline you wish to cut. Practically any paper that can be cut easily can be used but the most popular for stage work is tissue paper, and for impromptu performances, good old reliable newspaper, because it can be torn easily.

THE TORN AND RESTORED NEWSPAPER

This is a classic trick among magicians and many different ways have been devised to achieve the effect. This method is one of the best. The effect is that a double sheet of newspaper is torn into small squares. These squares are now opened out and it is seen that the newspaper has been completely restored to its original condition.

TO PREPARE

The secret of this effect is that you actually use two identical sheets of newspaper although only one of them is apparently seen by the audience. The properties you require for this effect are simple. Two identical sheets of newspaper, some glue or paste and a rubber band. Fold one of the newspapers up into a small packet, as shown in the illustration, and place a rubber band around this packet which should measure approximately three inches square. Open out the other sheet of newspaper,

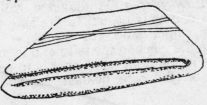

99

lay it out flat on a table top and paste the small packet as shown. While you are about it, it would be a good idea to make up several of these packets and paste them up to other duplicate sheets of paper so that you have a number of them all ready to practise with. Remember, every time you perform this effect you will have to prepare it first and this applies to practise also. Once the paste is dry fold the newspaper up with the prepared packet inside.

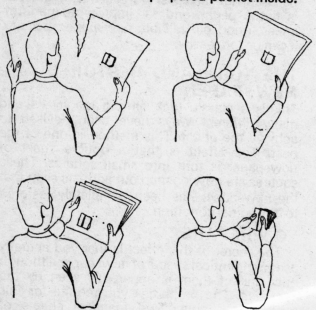

TO PERFORM

In performance you pick up the newspaper and open it out making sure that no one sees the small packet which is attached to it, by holding that side of the paper towards your body and away from the audience. Note that the small packet is pasted to the side that is held by the right hand. Tear the paper in two and place the piece in the left hand in front of the piece in the right hand, that is to say you place it on the side nearest the audience.

You may now tear the two pieces in half making four pieces and once again the pieces in the left hand are placed at the front. Once again you tear, and yet again and each time the left hand pieces are placed at the front until you have torn the paper into a number of small pieces approximately the same size as the small packet.

Place the two thumbs under the rubber band and lift it up off the folded packet, and over the torn pieces. Turn the packet over so the pieces are on the side closest to your body. Start to unfold the packet being careful not to expose the pieces which are now attached to the paper by means of the rubber band. For close quarter work it would be advisable to use a white rubber band but should you decide to perform this on a platform or stage any old rubber band will do.

This effect must not be performed with a light shining behind you because the small packet pasted to the rear of the paper will cast a shadow and give the game away. The same rule applies to performing in front of a window with daylight streaming through.

A Puzzle

Ask someone if he can draw a circle with a dot in the centre on a piece of paper, but he must not at any time lift the point of the pencil from the paper, and the use of an eraser is not allowed.

At first glance this may appear difficult but try it according to the illustrations. Fold the paper over, place the point of the pencil on the paper exactly at the point where the folded

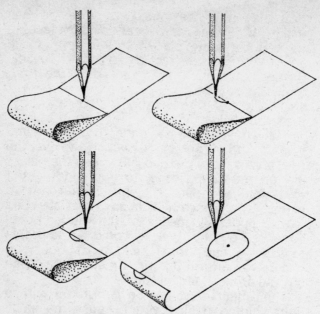

over end touches it, and from there bring the pencil on to the folded over portion. Move the point of the pencil along a little and off the folded over portion and back on to the other section of the paper. Flatten out the folded portion. From now on it is simply a matter of drawing a circle around the dot.

Fly away Peter, Fly away Paul

The effect about to be described is particularly suitable for showing to young children. You can get them to recite the little rhyme with you as the effect takes place. Take two small pieces of paper about the size of a dime and stick them to the fingernails of your forefingers, one on each hand. Place the two forefingers on the edge of a table and recite the following rhyme.

Two little dicky birds sitting on a wall
One named Peter, one named Paul
Fly away Peter, fly away Paul,
Come back Peter, come back Paul.

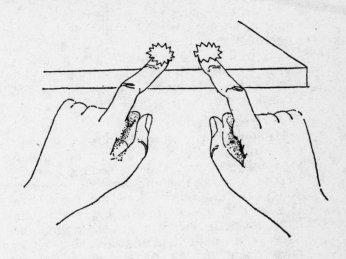

As you recite the rhyme the pieces of paper disappear and reappear one at a time in keeping with the rhyme as you recite it. The method is extremely simple.

Two little dicky birds sitting on a wall: Place forefingers on edge of table.

One named Peter: Tap left forefinger on table.

One named Paul: Tap right forefinger on table.

Fly away Peter: Lift up left hand to about head height and as you do so curl the forefinger into the hand and open middle finger and bring it down on to the edge of the table.

Fly away Paul: Repeat as above with right hand.

Come back Peter: Change fingers as before so that the forefinger comes down on the table.

Come back Paul: Repeat as above with the other hand.

The Magic Circles

YOU WILL NEED

For this effect you will require three long strips of paper three inches by forty inches. The easiest way to obtain paper of this length is to use old lining paper which is used for lining ceilings before decorating. If you have none of this available from the last time your family did the decorating you will have to buy some from your local wallpaper stockist. Fortunately, because it is plain white on both sides, it is the cheapest of all the papers.

TO PREPARE

Having got your three lengths take one of them and stick the two ends together making a complete circle. Take the second one and stick the ends of this one together, but before doing so, turn one end of the paper over. This is one reason for having plain white paper on both sides. If you used normal wall paper with a pattern on one side this twist you have made in the paper would be very noticeable. The illustration shows this second circle with the twist. The third strip is given a double twist before the ends are fixed together.

TO PERFORM

You now have three circles of paper which you can hold up for all to see. You should now realise the reason for the circles being so large. The twists in the papers are less noticeable the larger the circle. Show all three circles separately and lay them down on your table for a moment. Explain that you are going to have a paper cutting competition and offer to demonstrate what the competitors will have to do. Pick up the circle which has no twists in it and start cutting by inserting the point of the scissor blades through the paper and cutting in a continuous line around the circle until you have cut it into two complete and separate circles. Hold them up.

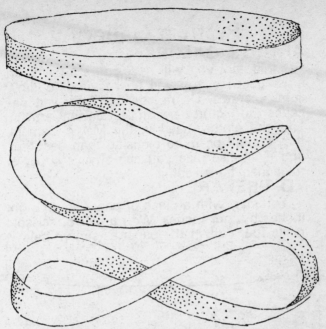

Ask for two volunteers to help you. Give one circle of paper to each and a pair of scissors to cut the circles. Explain that on the word of command they must start cutting and the first one to cut their paper into two complete and separate circles will be the winner. In actual fact, neither of them will be the winner, because neither of them will actually be able to cut their papers into two complete and separate circles. The person who is cutting the paper with one twist in it will finish up with one very large circle of paper and the person who has the paper with the double twist will finish up with two circles as required but he will be disqualified because his circles are not two separate circles, they are in fact linked together.

If you perform this for a very large audience a better plan is to have each person cut their papers separately and check how long each takes. This way the audience get more time to appreciate what has happened and the situation is more amusing and more prolonged.

Picture Gallery

ARTISTS GALORE

For this item you will have to be a bit of an artist because you will be required to draw some pictures. Do not despair however, because the pictures needn't be all that artistic. Like the picture used in the Magic Camera, they should be more amusing than beautiful, and if all else fails you can always copy, or trace them from a comic.

TO PREPARE

You start with a piece of paper about eight inches by four inches. With a pair of scissors make four cuts in the paper as shown below.

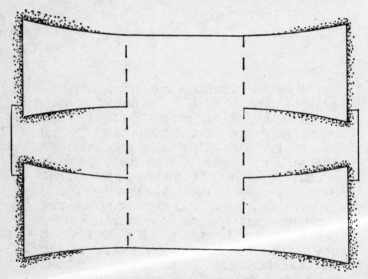

You will find it will help if you fold the paper in the creases shown first and cut to where the creases appear in the paper. You will now have the centre section of the paper intact and three pieces, or flaps, on either side of this centre section. At this stage you should fold the flaps back and forwards from front to rear so that they are reasonably loose, because this is their function.

With the paper prepared in this fashion we come to the artistic part of the operation. As the paper is lying on the table in front of you, fold the top left hand flap and fold it inwards on to the centre section; now fold the bottom right hand flap inwards also. Press them down firmly so that they will stay in position.

Start to draw a picture covering all three pieces of paper which now comprise the centre section. Having drawn this first picture, open the flaps out flat again and fold the bottom left hand and the right centre flaps inwards on to the centre section. Now draw a completely different picture on the three pieces which now comprise the centre section. If the first picture was a clown, make the second picture a soldier. Now fold in the top right and centre left sections and draw a schoolboy perhaps.

By now you should realise that the heads in these illustrations should all be in a central position. Up to now, you have drawn three pictures, clown, soldier and a schoolboy. Open out all the flaps so that the whole sheet of paper is lying flat on the table. Now turn it over from left to right, so that although you have turned the paper over, the pictures you have already drawn are still the right way up.

Now start drawing and folding all over again. Fold the top left and bottom right sections into the centre and draw a football player. Having done this open the flaps out and fold in the bottom left and right centre flaps and draw a picture of a chef. Open the flaps out and fold in the top right and centre left sections and this time draw a schoolgirl. That is the last drawing.

THE EFFECT

You now have a piece of paper with lots of pictures on it in what is apparently a jumbled mess. But if you fold some of the sections into the centre and some of them backwards around the rear of the paper so that they are out of sight, and only the centre sections are showing at the front, you will always get a complete picture. Some of the pictures will appear normal, but some of the others will be a combination of two or three drawings.

Funny Pictures

AUDIENCE PARTICIPATION

Take a sheet of paper and divide it up into six equal parts by folding it and creasing it as in the illustration. When the paper is opened out the creases should be clearly visible as dividing marks. Give the paper to someone and ask him to draw a head in the top division only. It can be any kind of head, male, female, fish, animal, but it must be discernible as a head and not an abstract picture which is supposed to represent a head. No one must see what this person has drawn and when he has finished he is to fold the top division backwards out of sight.

The paper is now given to a second person who is asked to draw a picture of a pair of shoulders and arms in the second division and when the picture is finished he is to fold the second division backwards out of sight.

You have probably realised what is to happen from now on. A third person draws a waist in the third section and folds it back, a fourth person draws that section of the body from the hips down to below the knees and finally a fifth person draws a pair of feet in the fifth section and folds it back so that all that can be seen is the last section which is blank.

Now ask all those who have contributed to the work of art if they would give a name to the finished picture and no doubt after a short discussion which will probably include

the names of several well known personalities or even friends, they will decide upon one name which you write in the last section.

After a short discourse on the merits of modern art you prepare to unveil the most recent addition to the National Portrait Gallery. Announce the name which has been chosen and with a flourish unfold the paper to reveal the composite work.

It can turn out to be amusing, ludicrous, ridiculous, describe it any way you like, they will all like it, and boast that their own particular contribution was the one that really put it into the Rembrandt class.

A Balancing Trick

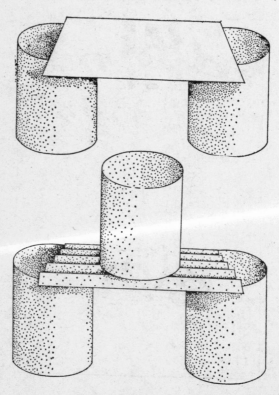

Place two glasses on the table, mouth upwards and balance a one dollar bill across the top. Ask a friend if he can now sit a third glass on the one dollar bill and balance it there without any other support.

Take the note and fold it several times in an accordian pleat and lay it across the two glasses and you will find that you can, quite easily, balance the glass there without any other means of support. Use a nice crisp note if possible.

Pure Skill

THE EFFECT

Pure Skill is the name given to this effect, because that is exactly what it looks like. There does not, at any time, appear to be any room for trickery. It seems to a spectator that you tear off a small strip of paper from a newspaper, and hold it at arms' length in the left fingers. The right hand is at your side holding a pair of scissors. The left hand releases its hold on the paper and as the paper flutters to the ground the right hand lunges at it and with a quick snip of the scissors, cuts a piece off the end of the paper.

If you will read that again you will see that this is what it LOOKS like. It is even possible that with a lot of practise you might, one day, be able to perform this effect, but there is no real need to waste a lot of time practising something which can be learnt in a few minutes with just a little chicanery.

TO PREPARE

Once again the picture tells all. A small strip of paper is concealed between the blades of the scissors. Needless to say, the broader the blades of the scissors the larger can be the piece of paper.

TO PERFORM

As soon as the left hand drops the paper, the right hand reaches forward and opens and closes the scissors quickly to give a snipping sound. The action of opening the scissors will release the concealed piece of paper, which will flutter to the floor with the original piece of paper and look as if it had just been snipped off the end.

Your immediate reaction to reading the above may be to try and get hold of as large a pair of scissors as possible to ensure a large piece of paper being concealed. There is no need to take the trouble, any scissors will do. If they will only conceal a small piece of paper, the answer is to drop a piece of paper which is not much larger and it will look as if you have almost cut it in two equal parts.

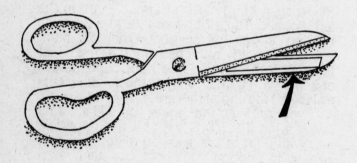

One last point. As long as you make the snipping action somewhere close to the falling piece of paper the illusion will be perfect. Do not try to get too close to it or you may finish up with the concealed piece fluttering to the floor and the other piece trapped between the blades of the scissors.

The Magic Tube

THE EFFECT

A large sheet of paper is shown to be completely free from deception. The performer forms it into a tube and after making the necessary magical incantations he proceeds to produce from within the tube a number of sweets, handkerchiefs, or, in fact, anything which the tube can hold. The Magic Tube is really the type of trick to perform in a set Magic Show rather than as an almost impromptu effect.

TO PREPARE

You will need a large sheet of paper about 24 inches by 24 inches and it should be fairly stiff paper and not floppy like newspaper. This sheet of paper should be folded in half and creased very firmly then rolled into a tube, fairly tightly and held in this position with a few rubber bands. This rolled up tube should now be left in this position for 24 hours. At the end of this time when you remove the rubber bands you will find that the paper will retain its form and still remain rolled up.

You now require a cardboard tube about 14 or 15 inches long by 1½ or 2 inches diameter. Unroll the paper, but still keeping it folded in half, and glue the cardboard tube in position as shown on page 54. You can either use some form of glue or strips of adhesive tape. Having done this, attach a strip of adhesive tape across one end of the tube. Your preparation is now complete and if you release the paper it should immediately roll up into a tube again, forming itself around the cardboard tube which is now concealed inside. Fill the cardboard tube with handkerchiefs, sweets etc. and you are ready.

TO PERFORM

It is impossible to show both sides of the paper before you make your production, but

you must make it appear as if that is what has happened.

Hold the tube in the left hand with the fingers inserted in between the two ends of the paper. The right hand reaches around in front of the roll and takes hold of one end of the paper and, at the same time, the left thumb and fingers take a grip on the other end of the paper. If you now move the left hand to the left and the right hand to the right, so that you are separating the hands but still holding the paper, the paper will be opened out to its full extent. Keeping a firm grip with the left hand, release the end that is being held in the right hand and the paper will immediately fly back to your left hand again and once more form itself into a roll around the cardboard tube.

To recap for a moment, you will see that what you have done is to take a rolled up piece of paper, open it out, let go of one end and the paper has rolled itself up again into a tube. You will have to try this for yourself in front of a mirror but it is the freedom with which you handle the paper and allow it to roll up again which convinces your spectators that there cannot possibly be anything concealed in the paper. You can make your production immediately.

If you intend to use this often the edges of the paper should be reinforced with adhesive tape to ensure a longer life.

TWO SIDES TO THE STORY

One other point which we have saved till last. Should you decide to include this effect in your regular repertoire, try to obtain paper which is a different colour on each side, as this will enhance the effect considerably. If the paper is blue on one side and pink on the other, when the paper is in its rolled up condition the audience will see a blue tube. When you open out the paper they will see a pink sheet of paper. When you release it and it rolls up they will once again see a blue tube. What you have done is make the audience think that they have seen both sides of a sheet of paper. They have seen the blue side and they know there is nothing concealed there. How can there be? It's the OUTSIDE of the tube. When you open it out and they see the pink inside, then, as far as an audience is concerned, they have seen both sides of the paper.

Finger Puppets

These are some of the simplest and most amusing novelties you can make for the entertainment of young children. Use stiff paper or thin card. Draw the picture in thick bold lines using a felt-tipped pen. If you are artistically inclined, paint one in full colour.

This puppet is amusing to adults and can actually be used as a Christmas card with an appropriate greeting on the back. All forms of puppets should be animated to make them really effective. Dance the puppet along the edge of a table top. When it reaches the edge make out he is falling, grab hold of him with the other hand and pull him back upwards on to the table top. Wear one on each hand and make them perform a dance together. Put thimbles on your fingertips and let the puppets tap dance to a record player.

A Magic Notebook

TRIM THE PAGES

Take a notebook — practically any notebook will do, but a small pocket type is best because you can carry it around with you. With a pair of scissors trim about $\frac{1}{16}$ inch off the edge of the *second leaf* all the way from top to bottom. Now repeat this with the *fourth leaf*, then the *sixth leaf* and so on throughout the whole notebook. Every *second leaf* from one end of the book to the other is trimmed a little shorter than the remaining pages. The *last* page in the note book should be a short one.

WRITE IN THE BOOK

Now open the notebook. Ignore the page which would be numbered one, in a novel, turn to page two, so that you have a long page on the left and a short page on the right. Fill in both of those pages with writing. Anything will do, names and addresses of your friends, instructions for making a model aeroplane, cookery recipes, anything at all that comes into your head. Having filled up those two pages with scribbles, turn over the short page, AND the next page which is a long one. This will now give you a long page on the left as before. Once again fill in both of those pages with writing. Turn two pages again and fill in with writing and so on throughout the book. When you leaf through the book, the first page should be blank, then two with writing then two blank, two with writing etc.

NOW YOU SEE IT – NOW YOU DON'T

Take hold of the book in the centre of the spine with *the right hand* and with the left thumb riffle the pages from the back of the book to the front. As the pages flick by, you will only be able to see the short pages therefore the book will appear to be full of writing. But if you take hold of the book at the centre of the spine with the left hand and flick the pages from front to back with the right thumb, you will only see the long pages, therefore the book will appear to be full of blank pages only.

VANISH SOME STAMPS

This same principle can be applied to other books besides notebooks. A stamp album can be treated in a similar fashion so that the pages can first be shown blank and the book can then be placed aside while you vanish some foreign stamps. When the book is taken up again it can be shown to be full of stamps. Instead of writing or stamps, use a colouring book. The pages can be shown in black and white first then after a suitable magic spell or incantation, the pictures can be shown to be coloured.

Moving Pictures

A FAST FLICK

In the days before cinema and television there was another form of moving pictures called the Magic Flick Book. Usually these books are quite small because the pages flick by much faster in a small book than they do in a book with large pages. About two inches square is ideal.

START YOUR PICTURES

Take a dozen or more pages of stiffish paper and lay them in a row on the table. On the first one draw an old fashioned chimney. On the second one draw the chimney with a chimney sweeps brush sticking out of it. On the third page draw the chimney and the brush plus a top hat. On the fourth, add a face to the top hat and on the next the shoulders of the chimney sweep.

This has taken five pages. On the sixth page, repeat the picture on the fourth page, on the seventh page repeat the third page, and so on until you have the picture of the chimney only, again. If you wish, you can repeat the whole sequence again. Starting with the last one first, place all the pages one on top of the other to form a small book, and either staple all the pages together or stitch them. If you now hold the book (for that is what it is now) at the spine between the forefinger and thumb of the left hand and flick through the pages from front to back, with the right thumb, you will see a chimney sweep bobbing up and down in a chimney pot.

Many other subjects will be found suitable for this treatment — a blacksmith hammering on an anvil, a gentleman doffing his top hat, a Jack in the Box popping up and down in a box with the lid opening and closing as he does so. Silhouettes are easy and visually satisfying, too. Try it, it's fun.

A MATCHSTICK MAN

If you have an old book at home, one that is about to be discarded, rescue it quickly and you can make yourself a moving picture outfit in a few minutes. In the corner of each page, draw the figure of a man running. Just draw straight lines so that he will be in effect, a Matchstick Man. Draw the arms and legs of the man in different positions so that when you flick through the corner of the book you will see him running. If there are a lot of pages in the book you can have him come up against several obstacles, such as a fence which he jumps over, or a stone which he kicks out of the way.

Make him change direction slightly so that he runs off into the distance. This is achieved by drawing the pictures progressively smaller until you can get right down to a little dot and finally he disappears into the far off horizon.